A Time of Hope

Margaret Ehlen-Miller
Rev. Robert Miller
Loretta VanderVeen
Carl VanderVeen

Illustrated by
Judy Winkowski

4/01
Morehouse-Barlow Company, Inc.
Wilton, Connecticut

TO:

Margaret and John
Betty and Gerald

ACKNOWLEDGMENTS

Those Bible passages marked GNB are taken from THE GOOD NEWS BIBLE, Today's English Version, copyright © American Bible Society, 1966, 1971, 1976, and are used by permission.

Those Bible passages marked NAB are taken from THE NEW AMERICAN BIBLE copyright © 1970 by the Confraternity of Christian Doctrine, Washington, D.C. and are used by permission of the copyright owner. All rights reserved.

Copyright © 1979
Margaret Ehlen-Miller, Robert Miller, Loretta VanderVeen, Carl VanderVeen and Judy Winkowski

Morehouse-Barlow Co., Inc.
78 Danbury Road, Wilton, CT 06897

ISBN—0-8192-1247-4

Printed in the United States of America

Table of Contents

LENT

EASTER

Introduction

Time is a powerful thing. It trains us to hope. It teaches us to experience the joy of living. In the form of anticipation, it helps us to put up with difficult or presently unpleasant things. The waiting of Lent can give us both the time and the energy to cleanse ourselves for newness. And when the expected time, Easter, arrives, we can truly pause to enjoy, celebrate and prolong moments of peace and fulfillment.

This book of activities for the Lenten-Easter seasons is given to families young and old. It contains practices and customs of the Church's celebration of this holy season: some familiar, some new, some international and many which we hope will become a treasured part of your family's "holy times for holy people."

Lent

There's an old story
about a day when Jesus cornered Peter with the question,
    "Do you love me?"
Three times he asked,
    "Do you love me, love me, love?"
Like Peter, we all want to say,
    "Yes, of course!"
        But times of impatience, of anger, or betrayal
        sound the depth of our hearts
            and reveal the unsureness of our minds,
                    of our purpose,
                    of our hearts.

        Even in the best of families,
          "Yes, of course"
            may be words rehearsed in the best of ways.
So each year Lent enters our lives,
    with ashes and sackcloth
        to stir up our hearts,
        to awaken our consciences,
        to shake our foundations
            and our assumptions.

Lent—Getting Started

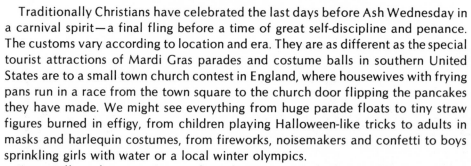

SHROVETIDE AND MARDI GRAS

Traditionally Christians have celebrated the last days before Ash Wednesday in a carnival spirit—a final fling before a time of great self-discipline and penance. The customs vary according to location and era. They are as different as the special tourist attractions of Mardi Gras parades and costume balls in southern United States are to a small town church contest in England, where housewives with frying pans run in a race from the town square to the church door flipping the pancakes they have made. We might see everything from huge parade floats to tiny straw figures burned in effigy, from children playing Halloween-like tricks to adults in masks and harlequin costumes, from fireworks, noisemakers and confetti to boys sprinkling girls with water or a local winter olympics.

Essentially, what constitutes the religious part of Shrovetide (time to be "shriven" or set to penance) are the two elements of "taking leave" of festivity and that of symbolizing our inner nature with jest, games, costumes, masks, and papier-maché figures.

The following family activities are designed around these elements.

A SHROVE TUESDAY PANCAKE DINNER

Families traditionally eat pancakes for Shrove Tuesday dinner. In the olden days of Lenten abstinence from meat, this was the last chance to use up scraps of meat and fat. Your family might make pancakes with this "use up" recipe.

1 cup bread crumbs
1 cup flour
1 teaspoon salt
1¾ teaspoons baking powder
2 eggs
3 Tablespoons bacon drippings (or butter)
1-1¼ cup milk

Directions:

Put in a mixing bowl:
1-1¼ cup milk
2 eggs
3 Tablespoons bacon drippings (or butter)
Beat lightly and quickly add to the milk mixture:
1 cup flour
1 cup bread crumbs (grind in a blender or crush with a rolling pin)
1¾ teaspoons baking powder
1 teaspoon salt
Stir until batter is well blended. If necessary, add enough milk to make the batter about as thick as heavy cream.

Serve with chicken and salad to complete the meal.

To give the meal an air of mystery and excitement, try hiding little "gifts" in the pancakes. Be sure to sterilize these items by boiling in water. Here are some ideas you might want to try, along with the meaning the gift symbolizes for the lucky recipient.

Ring—the person who receives this is soon to marry
Button—this person will get new clothes
Coin—wealth and riches for this person
Medal—this person will be involved in ministry
Paper clip—this person is scholarly and will become a writer

To insert "gifts" in pancake, pour batter onto heated griddle or frying pan. Allow the pancake to cook for a minute or two before adding "gift", then after bubbles have formed flip and cook reverse side. Mix pancakes with gifts in them with the rest made in a normal manner.

Stage a party or home carnival using some of these items:

—Old Christmas wrapping paper to make confetti
—Parts of old toys for a ring toss or penny throw
—Unused gadgets for a fishing pond or wishing well
—Scraps of old material for jester's costumes

As you plan ahead of time for the party, make clear the concept of using up or using for the last time some of the foods, toys, etc. For example, you might allow each child to buy something special on that day for the party with the understanding that during Lent extra monies will be put aside for the cause of your family's choice.

MASK-MAKING

For a more simple Mardi Gras celebration, each family member might make a self-mask to wear to dinner that night. The mask (see directions below) is made to symbolize how that person feels on entering the season of Lent. Choices of masks could be:

fox—to show that he wants to be tamed
clown—to show that he wants to be happier
ant—to show that he wants to be more industrious
tortoise—to show that he wants to slow down
flower—to show that he wants to grow and be more
   open

Use the beginning of dinner time to ask family members to explain their masks. After dinner, accompany each family member to his room to hang up his mask in a prominent place to remind him of his Lenten resolution.

Directions for Mask-making

Any recyclable items around the house are good for making masks. A brown paper bag with a cone-shaped, construction paper nose would make a fine start for a "fox" mask. A paper plate with crepe paper petals for a "flower" mask.
Some other suggested materials are:

Old wrapping paper
Colored tissue
Felt tip pens
Straws
Pipe cleaners
Net
Buttons
Artificial flowers
Scraps of material
Paper cups
Styrofoam packing material
Yarn

BURYING THE SARDINE

Mardi Gras in the South usually ends with a ceremony called "burying the sardine," which is really the burial of a strip of meat to symbolize the end of festivities. Your family might choose a portion of their favorite food to bury in symbol on Shrove Tuesday evening. Other ways to bring an end to festival include:

—a marathon dance (of at least a half hour's duration) at the end of which participants sink down to the floor as if in total exhaustion;

—the burning of the masks or papier-mâché figurines;

—the singing of a party song followed immediately by a song of mourning.

FAMILY FORGIVING TIME

Lent is a time of looking within ourselves to see just how concerned we might be for one another. Can you think of times when you might have treated a mother, brother, sister, father, husband, wife, friend, or even a stranger, in a more loving, caring manner? How easy it is to get angry at members of our family, especially "someone who bugs us all the time." Or how often we might tease another because "he had it coming!" As a result, love is lost, people are hurt, and there is a need for healing.

Many times when we hurt each other, we apologize and are forgiven. But other members of the family who may have witnessed the original scene are not present when the reconciliation takes place. So it seems important for the family to get together and spend part of an afternoon or evening reflecting on how they sometimes fail to support, care, and love one another. Then, in sharing forgiveness, they may receive a blessing or prayer.

Agree on a setting that is comfortable for all. For example, the family could be sitting on pillows on the floor by the fireplace or sitting around the dining room table. You will also need some strips of writing paper and pens or pencils, a candle, and a large ashtray or similar dish.

Try to find a time that is convenient for all family members so that no one is excluded.

Begin the ceremony by lighting the candle and sitting quietly for a minute or two. Then say this prayer or make up your own.

OPENING PRAYER

Lord, you told us to love one another
But the day is long
And living with others is so hard.
Little things bother us, we grate on each other's
  nerves.
Impatience creeps into our being.
Tempers flare, arguments spring forth,
And we end up hurting someone.
Lord, you also told us to forgive one another.
How wise you are!
For it is in the forgiving that
We set each other free to love fully once again.
Thank you, Lord, for bringing us together
So that we may heal and be healed.
                                        Amen.

Take a minute and reflect on yourself and how you might have been more loving, supportive, and caring for those in your own family.

Take the slips of paper and write or draw some of the ways you want to be forgiven.

For example, a father might write to his teenage daughter:

"Please forgive me for getting so angry with you when you came home late the other night. What I really needed to tell you was that I was scared because I was afraid something bad had happened to you. For this, I am very sorry."

Or a little boy might write to his sister:

"I'm sorry for making you cry by calling you a dirty ol' rat."

Write to as many people as you want or agree beforehand which person you want to write to. Care should be taken to include everyone. You may even want to write a slip to the whole family.

There are several ways you may use the slips.

First, you can share what you have written with the person you wrote to. (Some people who are a little uncertain or shy might not want to share at all and

that is all right.) Or, you can stand up before your entire family and read your request for forgiveness.

After you have received forgiveness, crumple your paper and drop it into the ashtray. (Be sure they are crumpled loosely so they will burn well.)

Reader:

These papers represent our sorrow
but we have forgiven and been forgiven,
so we want to put these sorrows behind us.
Let us get rid of them so we can have a fresh start.

Light one of the papers from the candle and use it to light the others in the ashtray. While they burn, read:

If you forgive others the wrongs they have
done you, your Father in Heaven will also
forgive you. But if you do not forgive the
wrongs of others, then your Father in heaven
will not forgive the wrongs you have done.
                              (Matthew 6:14-15 GNB)

Blow out the candle and give everyone a big hug. You all deserve it!

Now a closing prayer:

CLOSING PRAYER

Lord, thank you for being here with us today.
We are your servants, Lord, and try as we might
  to follow you, we stumble, falter along the way.
We came together today to help each other, to
  forgive and heal.
We have learned to grow a little closer and in
  so doing, we find you, too, Lord, are a little
  closer to each of us.
Lord, thank you for being here with us today.
                                        Amen.

THE MEANING OF ASHES

To most of us, ashes are the remains we find in the fireplace, in the ashtray, at a campout or in the barbecue after a picnic. To ancient peoples and to the people of God of the Old Testament ashes took on some very important meanings. Abraham spoke to the Lord in this way: *"See how I am presuming to talk to my Lord, even though I am but dust and ashes"* (Genesis 18:27 TNAB). Job sat down in the ashes to mourn and to do penance. Those who wished to do penance wore sackcloth and sprinkled ashes on their heads. Many times it was the duty of the priests to gather up the ashes. To these people, ashes represented their own lowly state in contrast to the greatness of God. God could make ashes of their enemies, so God had the same power over them. Ashes meant helplessness, a dependency on God who could do all things. It was from all these customs and concepts that many churches chose to use ashes on Ash Wednesday to begin the season of Lent. Ashes are blessed—they are made from the palms of the previous Palm Sunday—and smeared on the foreheads of those wishing to receive them in the sign of the cross with the words: "Remember that you are dust and to dust you shall return."

Here are some family activities you can use to carry out the Church's custom of using ashes during Lent.

—Your family might do its own ash blessing by burning pieces of palm saved from the previous year and signing each other on the forehead with the sign of the cross, using a statement remembering the meaning of Lent. Here are some examples: "remember that today you begin a new season of penance and self-discipline;" "remember that the things you have are given to you to use by God;" "remember that you are given to the service of God and not to selfishness."

—Charcoal pictures are a good use of ashes. Use the ends of corks from wine bottles. Burn them slightly until they are black ash color and then use them as markers to draw. Ask each family member to draw a scene from the passion of Jesus—for example, the carrying of the cross, the weeping women, the towel Veronica offers to Jesus.

—Ashes can be made from slips of paper on which each family member has written a habit or trait he wants to eliminate during the time of Lent. Or use the ashes from "Family Forgiving Time."

—Ink can be made from a mixture of ash and water. With a brush, pen or quill, each member of the family might write out a Lenten resolution using the ink from the ashes. (If the homemade ink is not dark enough, add India ink or black food coloring.)

TAKING LEAVE OF THE ALLELUIA

The Church has the custom of not speaking or singing the word "Alleluia" during Lent. "Alleluia" is one of the church's favorite words because it expresses joy, gives praise—it means "Praise the Lord"—and can be sung easily in so many different ways. Not using the word "Alleluia" during Lent is like putting away a

favorite toy for a while—to appreciate it better later. Here are some ways your family might observe the putting away of the Alleluia:

—Perhaps you have a recording of Handel's *Messiah* and play it at Christmas or Eastertime. If this is the case, have a last playing of the "Alleluia Chorus" just before Lent begins, and then wrap up the record and tie it with a purple bow (purple is the color of penance) to await its next playing on Easter Sunday.

—Each family member might choose one thing (toy, record, favorite piece of clothing, even the TV) to wrap up and tie with a purple bow not to be opened until Easter.

In many churches, along with the silencing of the Alleluia, comes the locking up of the organ, another custom of laying aside a good and beautiful thing so that it might be better appreciated later. The mood during Lent is often one of silence, offering us a time to listen instead to things we need to hear and say inside ourselves. Perhaps your family can make a list of ways to be more silent during Lent. It could include:

—The use of record players, radios, TV during only certain hours.

—Becoming conscious of things like slamming doors, noisy appliances, yelling from room to room.

—Creating a quiet hour each day at home. Note the use of the word "creating." It is important to understand that silence is not just the practice of cutting out noise and trying to keep quiet. Rather, it is a time when each person tries to make peace and quiet for each other. If you try it, you will most certainly *feel* the quiet you are making for each other.

THE PRACTICE OF WAITING

The Lenten Season lasts for forty days, or seven weeks. Often, this seems like a long time, longer than our waiting for Christmas. This is the time of year when we begin to wish winter would end, and spring would show itself sooner. Even though for adults the weeks seem to go fast, for children times like this can drag on and on. Children are just learning what it means to wait—to wait for a tooth to grow, to wait for a vacation time, to wait to be a year older. We can make Lent a time to practice waiting, to learn the meaning of time, and to experience perseverance in our Lenten resolutions.

Here are some suggested ways to help us all learn to wait.

—Take a tour of your house and see how many different objects you have for keeping track of time. Count your calendars, watches, clocks and even make a list of other things that tell you what time of the month or year it is. For example, the mail can tell you it is the middle of the month, the end of the month, time to get a dental check-up and so on.

—Sit down together and try to imagine and talk about what it must have been like before calendars and clocks existed, before people had so many ways to keep track of time. Or imagine what it is like to be three or four, the age where you don't yet know how long away your birthday is or when next week is going to come.

—The very early Christians had no calendars in their homes, and were not nearly as time-conscious as we are. When it came to Lent and they began a period of fasting and self-denial, naturally they would wonder when these forty days were coming to an end, or how far they had to go until the end. So they devised a special Lenten calendar to mark time—one that your family, too, might like to make. It is the figure of a woman. The woman has no mouth—indicating abstention from extra food during this time. She has her arms folded in prayer. She has seven feet to indicate the seven weeks of Lent. The figure is to be traced and cut out and hung on the wall, and at the end of each week, one of her feet is folded up. Your family's time of "folding up the foot" could be marked with any special kind of ceremony you create, for example, the recitation of a favorite Lenten prayer, taking turns to tell what the past week of Lent has meant to you, or a time of making a one-week resolution for the coming week. (Often one-week resolutions work better for us than forty-day ones.)

TEMPTATIONS OF JESUS

There are times in all of our lives when we are tempted. We are asked to stray from what we believe is right for us, to go against a conviction that we have. We are sometimes asked to reverse a decision we have taken time to arrive at. Perhaps we have decided to lose weight and we are invited to a gourmet dinner. We have been trying to quit smoking and somehow find ourselves in a room filled with smokers. A child may be struggling desperately with homework and is constantly distracted and tempted by sounds of other children playing. How easy it might be to say an unkind word to the neighbor who shouts to passers-by to keep off her property.

It is difficult to resist temptations. We resist at first, then hesitate, weaken, and finally surrender to our weakness. Jesus, too, was often tempted, but he firmly said "no" at such times.

Read: Matthew 4:1-11

The following activity, a stick-puppet show, demonstrates how difficult it is to resist temptation in a modern day setting.

Adjust the number of characters to those in your family. You might plan to share this activity with one or two other families.

THE MAGIC CHARM

Characters:

> NARRATOR
> BOY
> PARTY FRIEND #1
> PARTY FRIEND #2
> PARTY FRIEND #3
> RABBIT
> NEIGHBOR BOY
> SISTER

Scene I

NARRATOR: Our story begins at a lively birthday party. The children are all laughing and talking.

[On stage: Boy, Party Friends #1, #2, #3, and Neighbor Boy]

BOY: Look at this model! *(Examining present he has just opened)*

PARTY FRIEND 1: Wow!

PARTY FRIEND 2: Open this one. *(Motions to hand Boy small box)*

BOY: Okay *(opens present)*

PARTY FRIEND 3: Look, it's a rabbit's foot!

PARTY FRIEND 1: Rabbit's feet are supposed to bring good luck.

BOY: Yes. I've heard that. I wonder if this one will bring me good luck. Let's go outside.

(Puppets begin to exit slowly)

PARTY FRIEND 2: Hey, can I hold it? I could use some good luck.

PARTY FRIEND 3: Me too!

NEIGHBOR BOY: *(last one to leave)* That's dumb. Who'd believe a rabbit's foot could bring luck.
(exits)

Scene II

NARRATOR: Now, the boy carried the rabbit's foot with him wherever he went. He often dreamed that his rabbit's foot became part of a real rabbit.

(Enter Boy and Rabbit, frolicking together)

NARRATOR: The Boy and Rabbit grew to be good friends. He respected and loved the Rabbit. He talked to him when he was lonely and confided in him when he had troubles. The Rabbit seemed to be very wise in the ways of people and gave the Boy advice when he needed it. One day it became necessary for the Boy to go to the store on an errand.

(Exit Rabbit. Boy walks slowly across stage. Enter Neighbor Boy)

NEIGHBOR BOY: Hi. What are you doing?

BOY: *(hesitates)* I—I'm going to buy something.

NEIGHBOR BOY: *(impatiently)* Well, what's so important?

BOY: *(blurts out)* I'm going to buy a tube repair kit so I can fix my sister's bicycle tire.

NEIGHBOR BOY: *(laughing)* Fix your sister's tire! You've got better things to do than that!

BOY: Oh, but I promised her.

NEIGHBOR BOY: Aw, come on—we're getting a baseball team together. We could use you.

BOY: I'd love to . . . but, I really can't.

NEIGHBOR BOY: *(more impatiently)* Don't be silly. If you come, I'll pick you first to be on my team.

BOY: You will?

NEIGHBOR BOY: Sure.

BOY: Oh, but I promised—she's been waiting all day for me.

NEIGHBOR BOY: *(sighing)* Well, you're just going to miss out on all the pizza.

BOY: You're going to have pizza?

NEIGHBOR BOY: Yep, we're going to the pizza place afterwards. *(exits)*

BOY: Wow! I'd sure hate to miss that. *(starts to follow)*

(Enter Rabbit)

RABBIT: Your sister is really going to be disappointed.

BOY: Oh, I'll do it another day. It won't matter.

RABBIT: Don't you remember when we talked about hurting each other's feelings and keeping promises?

BOY: *(angry)* You can't play ball with promises or eat feelings!

RABBIT: *(patiently)* That may be true. But sometimes when it is so very hard to say no and then you do—you change—you become different inside.

BOY: I feel different inside all right. Look, he's gone. I've missed out. *(Exit Boy slowly looking dejected)*
RABBIT: But you really haven't missed . . . *(voice trails off, exits)*

Scene III

NARRATOR: That day the Boy repaired his sister's bike. The sweat poured down his brow as, at last, he fitted the tire back into the frame. His sister stood by and watched the whole time. Her little face reflected and mimicked each grimace and contortion on her brother's face as he did the job.
BOY: Whew. At last this thing is finished.
SISTER: *(excited voice)* Oh thank you! You don't know what this means to me. *(kisses Boy who backs away shyly)*
BOY: Aw . . . it was nothing. I would have done it sooner . . .
NARRATOR: But his sister did not hear him because she was already on her bike and riding off leaving the Boy standing there. Standing very tall and straight. He turned and walked into his house. Although he did not notice, he held his head a little higher and his step was lighter and stronger than it had ever been. He fingered the rabbit's foot in his pocket.

He decided to treat himself to a dish of ice cream.

PUPPET PATTERNS

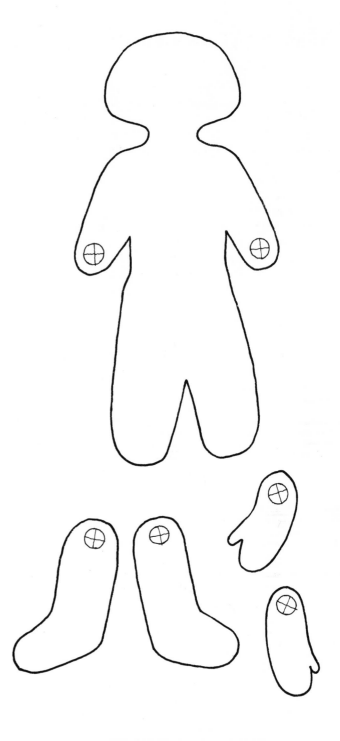

STICK-PUPPET DIRECTIONS

You will need to trace the basic puppet pattern six times onto lightweight cardboard. Cut out the puppets and punch holes where parts are to be joined. Fill in features and color in costumes to create the characters of Boy, three Party Friends, Neighbor Boy and Sister. Do the same with Rabbit. Fasten arms and legs to bodies with metal brads. Attach a plastic straw or thin wooden 10" dowel to the back of each puppet head with masking tape. Attach another to back of one hand. Hold a stick in each of your hands to make the puppet move.

12

Lent—The Understanding Time

THE WAY OF THE CROSS

It is the custom in Mexico and other places for everyone in a village or town to act out in a play the events of Good Friday—the trial before Pilate, the carrying of the cross from Pilate's Palace, out the gate of the city, and up the hill to the Place of the Skull, where Jesus was to be crucified. Everyone has a part to play— mothers, fathers, sisters, brothers. Seeing what happened to Jesus acted out makes that Friday of so long ago more real to us. We begin to understand how very much Jesus loved his family and friends, that he was willing to die for them —not merely for the people he knew in his life at that time, but for all of us, all who call Jesus our friend and our brother. That is what is said at our Baptism, that Jesus and we have a special relationship, a special friendship, like the love between brothers and sisters.

Your family can follow in the Way of the Cross any time during Lent, but especially on Good Friday, the day when the entire Church remembers the last day of Jesus' life. Each member of the family can play a part —there are many characters to choose from. Some members who are especially gifted with acting skills can play more than one part. If you need more "actors" you could invite another family to share in your Way of the Cross. Note that these stations are adapted for use at familiar family places, and so they are not the same stations as those used in church.

Cast of Characters

JESUS	CROWD (EVERYONE)
SEVERAL DISCIPLES	JESUS' MOTHER
JUDAS	SIMON
TWO SOLDIERS	VERONICA
PILATE	READER(S)

The First Station: In the Garden

Our first station can begin in the back yard or garden. Long ago Jesus went to the city garden, Gethsemane, in Jerusalem with his friends to pray. You can be there with your family. As the Bible tells us, after praying, one of the disciples, Judas, hugged Jesus— that was the signal for two soldiers to come out from their hiding places behind the bushes to arrest the Lord. Judas was part of a plot to trap Jesus. So, everyone in place. Action.

—Jesus and his disciples are praying.

—Judas comes up to Jesus and hugs him.

—Two soldiers come from behind the bushes and take Jesus by the arms.

As everyone is standing, a member of the family could read this prayer:

Lord Jesus, we remember here the good times you spent with your friends, the times

of healing and celebration, the times of prayer, and the times when some forgot how to love you. We, too, have known such moments in our family. May our love for one another always be the way to bring us together again. Amen.

The Second Station: Standing Before Pilate

Jesus was then taken before the Governor, Pilate, who was the judge in that region. Pilate had to decide if Jesus was guilty of leading a revolt against the Roman government. That was the charge made against Jesus. The prophecies in the Old Testament told of the coming of a king in the lineage of the famous warrior King David and this made many people expect that Jesus would overthrow the Roman rulers and again establish the independence of Israel. And so our drama unfolds, in your kitchen.

—Pilate asks Jesus, who is standing before him, "Are you king?"

—Jesus answers, "It is as you say, yes! But I am king of people's hearts."

—Pilate then says to the crowd (your family), "I find him guilty. What shall be done to punish him?"

—Everyone shouts, "Crucify him!"

Jesus is judged and sentenced to die. A member of the family can lead the prayer:

Lord Jesus, we remember the times when we have been misunderstood or accused of doing something we really didn't do. May the trust we share in our family help us to be patient and loving and not to be angry at such times. Amen.

13

The Third Station: Jesus Begins to Carry the Heavy Cross

After a night without any sleep or food, Jesus began the long hike through the city and out into the country-side. Some distance from town, near the main highway, was a hillside where he and two criminals would be crucified. We can begin our walk from the doorway to the house, which we can imagine to be the city gate. The person playing Jesus could carry a cross made of sticks or one that usually hangs on the wall. Everyone can follow.

—Jesus leads your entire family just a little distance into the garden.

Just as the mob was near the gates of Jerusalem (the gate to your yard), Jesus fell under the weight of the cross—because it was big and heavy.

—Jesus falls with his cross, but struggles to get up again.

—Reader:

Jesus, sometimes we get tired and irritable, some-times more tired than we think we are—and we make the way difficult for each other. May we learn patience with ourselves, to make an extra effort to help one another and to admit to others our lack of rest, in the hope that we may be forgiven.   Amen.

The Fourth Station: Jesus Sees His Mother

The first person Jesus recognizes is his mother. She was so saddened by what was happening that tears fell from her eyes. She loved her son very much.

—The mother of Jesus comes to him, sobbing.

—Jesus says,

"Mother, I love you very much. You have done so much for me. Thank you."

—Reader:

Jesus, you loved your mother very much and knew about the hurt she felt inside. Sometimes we hurt our mother by saying we don't care or by lying. But through all of that hurt mother's love for us shines. Thank you, Lord, for the steady love of a mother.   Amen.

The Fifth Station: Simon Helps Jesus Carry the Cross

The march to the hillside called Golgotha continued. Jesus was getting so very tired—each step was an effort. Suddenly, from the crowd that was following, Simon steps forth and helps Jesus to carry the cross the rest of the way.

—Jesus leads the procession to another part of the yard, (perhaps outside the garage). Each step becomes slower and slower, because he's tired.

—Simon the Cyrene steps forward and helps Jesus

to carry the cross to the next place. A prayer is offered:

—Reader:

Lord, the time when friendship is very special is when we need someone else to help us with the problems in our lives. Send your blessing upon our friends, our helpers in life.   Amen.

The Sixth Station: Veronica Wipes Jesus' Face

By now the work of carrying the cross was making Jesus perspire a lot. A friend, Veronica, steps forth from the crowd to wipe Jesus' face with a cool, damp cloth. How refreshing that must have felt to Jesus!

—Begin to walk back towards the house now.

—Veronica comes up to Jesus and wipes his face with a damp washcloth.

—Reader:

There are so many ways, Lord, when we can refresh one another. Just holding hands, or getting one another a cool glass of water on a hot day, or rubbing someone's back, or being with someone who is having a hard day can be ways of refreshing one another. Help us to know when someone needs us.   Amen.

The Seventh Station: Jesus Is Stripped of His Clothes

Our clothes both protect our bodies from the cold and from being cut or scraped by things we come into contact with. Jesus wore a long shirt on the way to Golgotha, but now the soldiers take it off him—to expose his skin to the cold and to let people see the marks from the whipping they had given him the night before.

—The "soldiers" remove Jesus' shirt. Then, with a red washable marking pen, they draw the marks of the whipping Jesus received earlier.

—Reader:

Jesus, as we see you stripped of everything you ever owned, help us to see that our clothes, our bodies, and our health are not our possessions but the gifts of God.   Amen.

The Eighth Station: Jesus is Nailed to the Cross

—Walk in procession back into the house to the living room, where there are some boards on the floor, placed in the shape of a cross. There is also a hammer and some nails.

—Reader:

Simon put the cross on the ground, and Jesus was ordered by the soldiers to lie on it, with his arms stretching outwards. Then one of the soldiers took

14

some nails and a hammer, and nailed Jesus' hands and feet to the wood. It must have really hurt, because we know how much even a splinter in a finger can hurt us.

—One of your "soldiers" can hammer some nails partly into the wood on the floor.

—Reader:

Lord Jesus, we can imagine how much the blows of the hammer must have hurt you, because we have often felt pain in our bodies, too. May we remember in such times that you let others hurt you because you loved them; perhaps our pain will then not feel so bad. Amen.

The Ninth Station: Jesus Dies

Jesus hung on the cross for three hours, from noon to three o'clock. Hungry, tired from the long walk, light-headed and feeling faint from the loss of blood from his wounds, Jesus died.

—Each member of your family can hold his or her arms out to the side, in the shape of a cross, for a minute of silence. You will begin to feel how heavy your arms can get, and so to feel something like the tiredness Jesus must have felt. When they get too tired, just let them drop to your sides.

—Reader:

Jesus, we have let our arms drop because our muscles were tired. We remember that your body relaxed as you died on the cross. We feel a bit rested now, which reminds us that death must be a kind of rest. Amen.

The Tenth Station: Jesus is Buried

—The family now goes to a bedroom.

Jesus' body was taken down from the cross by his friends and placed on a stone bed in a cave. In Jesus' time, people were buried in the many caves in the hills throughout Israel. A big rock was then rolled to block the entrance.

—Jesus can be helped to the bed, laid upon it, and covered with a sheet. Someone can close the door, blocking the entrance to the room.

—Reader:

And so, Jesus, you were buried by your mother and your friends. Sometimes we spend time in our rooms, to be there alone—to think or to read or to study or even to dream. Sometimes we may be sent to our rooms because we haven't been nice. But our time in our rooms is special to us, and we come out of them to greet our family and friends with gladness in our hearts. We remember that you came out of your tomb on Easter morning—to

be with your family and friends again, very much alive and glad to be with them. Amen.

—Each person leaves the room in silence and goes back to the cross for a few moments of reflection.

THE TIME OF THE AGONY OF JESUS

We know that in the last year of Jesus' life, time was very precious to him. He kept telling his friends that the time was near, the time for his delivery, for his agony, for his death. It is difficult for most of us to understand what this all meant—waiting *and* expecting the end to be painful—but we can know something of this feeling from our daily experiences. The following family evening is planned to help us take the time to understand Jesus' agony.

—Gather the family together before the usual dinner hour and begin by presenting this list of Bible references where Jesus tells his friends what he fears and what will come: Matthew 16:13-23; 17:22-23; 20:17-19; Mark 8:27-33; 9:30-32; 10:32-34; Luke 9:18-22; 9:44-45; 18:31-34. Send each person off with a Bible or with one or two of the quotes written down and a piece of blank paper and a pen. Ask him or her to be alone for twenty minutes to read the passage, to think about it, and then either to draw or write what Jesus must have felt about his coming time of suffering. (With younger children, have them pair off with older members to listen, talk and draw.) Gather everyone back together after the twenty minutes to share.

—Eat together, but tonight only bread and water. Talk about how you might this evening experience a bit of Jesus' suffering and the suffering of all peoples in the world by eating only bread, perhaps by using only flashlights or candles, turning down the heat in the house, and spending the evening in silence except for your times of prayer and sharing together.

—After dinner, lay out a collection of old newspapers and magazines. Ask each person to look for a current story of suffering to share. Take turns reading or telling the stories and then close with a prayer for each of the persons in suffering. Save these articles to paste on a cardboard or wood cross like a mosaic. On the reverse side, articles or pictures of joy and celebration could be glued and on Easter morning the cross could be turned around.

—Replay this drama of Jesus' agony in the garden.

Characters: Jesus, James, Peter, Narrator.

Use costumes and props if you wish, for example, bathrobes, head shawls, a small table for the rock in the garden. Use two rooms of the house—one for the entrance into the garden the other for Jesus to go farther on to pray. Use background music. Classical instrumental music seems best for setting a somber mood.

Narrator: Let us turn our thoughts this night to Jesus and to his feelings of loneliness, anguish and fear, remembering our own times of sorrow.

Jesus: I am afraid. Even though you are with me tonight, I feel alone. This night begins a dreaded time for me. I know that my enemies lie in wait for me. I am afraid. I want to go into the garden to pray. I want you to come with me, to be by my side.

Peter: What do you think he's talking about? We can easily hide from enemies. Everyone in town is celebrating; they're all drunk. We just have to stay away from the fights.

James: We'll be safe here in the garden. I think I'll take a nap.

John: Sure, we'll all be safe here. We can just rest the night. *(All three of them lie down and begin to drop off to sleep)*

Jesus: *(Turning to see them behind him)* My heart is nearly broken with sorrow. Stay awake with me and pray. *(Jesus kneels down; his friends are already sound asleep. After a long pause, seemingly in agony and very much afraid, he looks up and says)* My Father, if it is possible, let this cup pass me by. Still, let it be as you would have it, not as I. *(Short music interlude) (Jesus slowly rises and goes back to where his friends are asleep)* So you could not stay awake with me for even an hour? *(Then he walks back and kneels again)* My Father, if this cannot pass me by without my drinking it, your will be done. *(Short music interlude) (Again he walks back to his sleeping friends)* So you are still asleep, enjoying your rest. But the hour has come when the Son of Man is to be handed over to the power of evil men. Get up! Let us be on our way. See, my betrayer is already here. *(Friends slowly wake up and begin to follow Jesus out.)*

—Finally, talk about how afraid Jesus must have been that night, especially when his friends left him and he was really all alone. Ask each family member to tell about personally experiencing fear and loneliness. Talk about some people at work or school or in your neighborhood who might feel afraid or alone and decide what you can do about it.

THE SEVEN LAST WORDS OF JESUS

Many of the customs and concepts of the Church come in sevens. In addition to the list of the seven last words (phrases) of Jesus, here are several other uses of the number seven. Make a family study time of them. Give one list to each family member and ask him or her to take the time to study it, look up meanings of words, for example, and return to your family circle to say something or explain something about each of the seven items on the list.

THE SEVEN LAST WORDS OF JESUS (from The King James Version):

Father forgive them, for they know not what they do. (Luke 23:34)

Today shalt thou be with me in paradise. (Luke 23:43)

Woman, behold thy son! . . . Behold thy Mother! (John 19:26)

My God, my God why has thou forsaken me? (Matt. 27:46)

I thirst. (John 19:28)

It is finished. (John 19:30)

Father, into thy hands I commend my spirit. . . . (Luke 23:46)

THE SEVEN SORROWS OF MARY

The prophecy of Simeon (Luke 2:33-35)

The flight into Egypt (Matthew 2:13-15)

The loss of the Holy Child (Luke 2:41-52)

The meeting with Jesus on the way to Calvary (Luke 23:27-31)

Standing at the foot of the Cross (John 19:25-27)

Taking down the body of Jesus from the Cross (John 19:38-42)

The Burial of Jesus (Mark 15:46-47)

THE SEVEN VIRTUES

Faith
Hope
Charity
Justice
Prudence
Temperance
Fortitude

THE SEVEN GIFTS OF THE HOLY SPIRIT

Wisdom
Understanding
Counsel
Fortitude
Knowledge
Piety
Fear of the Lord

THE SEVEN DEADLY SINS

Pride
Covetousness
Lust
Envy
Gluttony
Anger
Sloth

To end your study, choose one of the penitential Psalms to read and recite from the Bible. Psalms 6, 32, 51, 102, 130, or 143.

FRIENDS WHO BETRAY US

One of our prized possessions is friendship. We spend time with friends sharing meals, going to movies, shopping, picnicking, laughing, crying, praying. A closeness develops. We seek out our friends to confide in or consult when problems arise. They can play a very important part in our lives. We love them in a very special way. Sometimes we do not realize how much they have meant to us until a time comes when they have let us down and all our expectations are shattered. When this happens, we might get a sick feeling inside and find ourselves moping aimlessly about the house.

Our friends can let us down or betray us in lots of different ways. In little things such as being late for a dinner date or forgetting to notice a new outfit or haircut or more important to us, perhaps, our friend has said an unkind word or revealed a special secret. Because we expect so much of our friends, it is a most difficult thing to understand and try to forgive them. When we deny forgiveness and understanding to our friends we deny Christ.

What a monumental task it must have been for Jesus to forgive the friends who betrayed him at the end. With death impending Jesus must have experienced great disappointment as his friends denied the bond they had shared for many months. How can we extend forgiveness to our friends?

Either alone or with another family try the following activity designed to bring us closer to our friends and to understand and try to accept disappointments in our friendships.

In the afternoon or day before:

— Make heart cookies or if you have a heart mold bake a heart cake.

— Assemble colored construction paper, scissors, glue, coat hangers, yarn or string, pens or pencils.

— Cut out enough hearts (using sample included) for each person to have at least one.

That night after dinner:

— Gather together in a comfortable setting with soft background music of your choice.

— Read the following scripture passages:

*He who is a friend is always a friend,
 and a brother is born for the time of stress.
 Proverbs 17:17. (TNAB)*

*Discuss your case with your neighbor,
 but another man's secret do not disclose.
 Proverbs 25:9. (TNAB)*

*A kind mouth multiplies friends,
 and gracious lips prompt friendly greetings.
Let your acquaintances be many,
 but one in a thousand your confidant.
 Sirach (Ecclesiasticus) 6:5, 6. (TNAB)*

*A faithful friend is a sturdy shelter;
 he who finds one finds a treasure.
A faithful friend is beyond price,
 no sum can balance his worth.
 Sirach 6:14, 15. (TNAB)*

— Pass out the paper hearts and pencils.

Mini Journal and Heart Mobile

Read the following incomplete sentences and ask individuals to write their response directly on the paper heart. You need not use names. Younger children may draw pictures of their friends and an incident appropriate to the evening's theme.

— The thing that is hardest about having you for a friend is _____, but I understand and forgive you.

— Give an example of when someone lets you down. I understand and forgive you.

— I was disappointed when you did not respond the way I expected you to. Like the time you _____ _____. I understand and forgive you.

Now glue the heart together (See pattern on p. 18) with the writing on the inside. Attach to string and arrange on coat hanger. Find a suitable place in the house for the mobile to be displayed.

A PRAYER FOR OUR FRIENDS

*Our friends make us feel warm and great inside.
They can brighten our day instantly.
Friends are the ones we look forward to doing all those
 special things with
Yet, Lord, sometimes they can really hurt us.*

4/01

They don't mean to
*   And they're sorry.*
But it hurts—because we love them so much.
Help us to be forgiving, Lord.
Help us to be loving, Lord.   Amen.

THE CROWN OF THORNS

In St. John's version of the Passion of Jesus it says: *The soldiers then wove a crown of thorns and fixed it on his head.* Almost every crucifix we see has Jesus pictured with a crown of thorns on his head. That crown of thorns has been preserved as a relic. It was kept first in Jerusalem, then in Constantinople and then in the thirteenth century King St. Louis IX of France built an entire chapel, which remains today as *La Sainte Chapelle de Paris,* to house the crown of thorns.

Crowns were often used in ancient times. Kings wore crowns of gold. Those who had won races and contests wore crowns of laurel leaves. And so it was fitting that Jesus wear some kind of crown, the crown that signified suffering.

Perhaps your family would want to make a kind of crown of thorns to display in your home during Lent and remind you of the victory over suffering. Here are some possibilities.

— Take rose stems or some other thorny vine; cut off the leaves and dampen the branches with the remaining thorns until they bend into a crown shape.

— If you live in a desert area, use any suitable kind of cactus that can be bent into the shape of a crown.

— Use a piece of wood cut in a ring or rounded shape and pound nails through the wood at different angles to look like thorns.

— Shape some barbed wire into a crown.

Here are some questions about thorns and crowns and pain you might use at a family prayer or discussion time:

What does the dictionary say a crown is?

Tradition says someone else must always crown a person. Why do you think this is so?

Where do you think the expression "I could crown him for doing that!" came from?

What does it mean when someone says, "He is a thorn in my side?"

Can you share any stories of how you experienced pain from a thorn from a plant? What is the difference between a thorn puncture and an ordinary cut?

Use this song to close your discussion:

O Sacred Head surrounded
By crown of piercing thorn
O Bleeding Head so wounded
Reviled and put to scorn.
Our sins have marred the glory
Of thy most holy Face
Yet angel hosts adore thee
And tremble as they gaze.

O Lord of every nation
Was hung upon a tree
His death was our salvation
Our sins, his agony
O Jesus, by thy Passion
Thy life in us increase;
Thy death for us did fashion
Our pardon and our peace.

FASTING

Bread, the staff of life, the symbol of life for mankind, has universal meaning for all peoples. Throughout history the mainstay of many cultures has been bread. Bread *is* life. It is easy to understand, then, why Jesus used it as a symbol at the Last Supper to say that we have food for our souls as well as for our bodies. He shared this symbol, bread, with his friends and asked that we do likewise in his name.

The sharing of bread with others and the idea of fasting seem compatible. How do we think of fasting in our own personal lives? Is it simply a giving up of some favorite treat traditionally done once a year during Lent, or is fasting a time to take a fresh look at what we think we need to consume? Is fasting a quick tool to lose ten pounds, or a means to some positive spiritual growth?

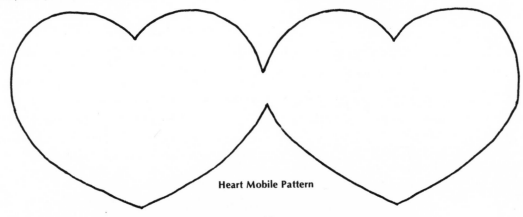

Heart Mobile Pattern

There are many ways to bring ourselves to a greater awareness of what our own needs and the needs of others are by limiting our daily intake, not only of food but of all natural resources. We can, for example, limit our use of water, electricity, paper products, etc. By limiting the amount of food we eat there will be more to nourish others.

It is hard to believe that in a world with such advanced technology many people have little or nothing to eat; not only in countries like Biafra and Bangledesh, but within our own cities as well. It is not a happy picture and we often feel overwhelmed and frustrated. Mother Theresa of Calcutta tells us, "If there are a hundred people to feed and you can only feed one—then feed one." There is much we can do through our own fasting as Christian families to reach out in a positive way to help others.

A FAMILY FOOD BOX

A large grocery-type box can be decorated by family members with drawings and pictures from magazines and local newspapers. Pictures of people sharing food together or helping one another would be appropriate. Glue these over the entire box, adding scripture quotes and Christian symbols if desired. At each evening meal during Lent select a wholesome, nonperishable food item from that evening's meal to go into the box. For example, if a menu included Tuna & Noodles, a can of tuna might be chosen. Each time this is done a special spontaneous prayer could be offered, such as:

FATHER, we care and are concerned about those who go hungry. We ask your blessing on this food that we are about to eat and which we share gladly with others. Amen.

By Holy Week the box should contain some good basic food items. Perhaps a canned ham could be added at the last for someone's Easter supper. Gather everyone together for a prayer of thanksgiving before delivering the box to a needy family. Or contact a local service agency such as St. Vincent de Paul, the Red Cross, United Way, or Salvation Army for distribution.

A Soup Supper

Another way for groups of families to share themselves and their food with others is a soup supper. Invite them to bring soup makings (rice, diced vegetables, beans, lentils, macaroni) prepared to go into a hot stock. The amount would be determined by the size of the group. While the soup is simmering for an hour or so, join in a shared prayer time using scripture and a favorite Lenten reading, or plan a slide presentation with appropriate music. The actual meal can consist of the soup and bread, with the amount one would have spent on a regular meal to be sent to your local charity or an international agency such as Operation Rice Bowl, Concern, or Care.

We are no longer Jews or Greeks, or slaves or free men or even merely men and women—we are Christians; we are one in Christ Jesus. Galatians 3:28

THE PRETZEL

The pretzel has been used during Lent for over fifteen hundred years. It is thought that originally pretzels were made by monks to resemble arms crossed in prayer. These breads were called "little arms." This can have deep spiritual meaning for us during Lent. Since basically only flour and water are used, pretzels can remind us of fasting. Here is a simple recipe. The entire family can participate in the baking. Why not invite another family over for an evening of shared baking and prayer?

SOFT PRETZELS

1 cake yeast dissolved in 1½ cup warm water
Add 1 teaspoon salt and 1 tablespoon sugar
Blend in 4 cups of flour

Knead dough until smooth. Cut into small pieces. Roll into ropes and twist into desired shape. Place on lightly greased cookie sheet. Brush pretzel with beaten egg. Sprinkle with coarse salt. Bake immediately at 425° for 12-15 minutes. (For hard pretzels use only 1¼ cups water and add ¼ cup melted butter. Shape smaller and bake until brown.)

PRETZEL PRAYER

Heavenly Father, we ask you to bless these little breads. Each time we eat them may we be reminded of the special season we are in and that through prayer we will become better people to each other. Let us not forget those who are in need of our prayers daily. Keep your loving arms around us, O Father, to protect us always. Amen.

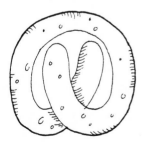

FAMILY HELP PROJECTS

"I was hungry and you fed me, thirsty and you gave me drink; I was a stranger and you received me in your homes; naked and you clothed me; I was sick and you took care of me; in prison and you visited me." The righteous will then answer him, "When, Lord, did we ever see you hungry and feed you, or thirsty and give you drink? When did we ever see you a stranger and welcome you in our homes, or naked and clothe you? When did we ever see you sick or in prison, and visit you?" The King will answer back, "I tell you, indeed, whenever you did this for one of the least important of these brothers of mine, you did it for me!"

Jesus tells us to reach out in service to others and to give them help and hope in times of need. Discuss how this message can also be a call for families to work together on special service projects. Some examples which might be tried are:

AN UNBIRTHDAY DAY

Many times someone in the family is in need of extra support. Set a day aside on which the rest of the family will give that person extra support by doing his or her chores, making his or her bed, picking up his or her room, cooking a favorite dinner and generally making the day special.

REACH OUT TO NEIGHBORS

1. Plan a neighborhood Easter egg hunt. Send out a notice about a week in advance to inform neighbors of details of the event and to bring colored eggs an hour or two before the actual time of the hunt. Older children can hide the eggs. Have a special silver and gold egg which gives the lucky finder an extra prize.

2. "Discover" the retired people in your neighborhood. Find out what their talents are and see how they may be shared. For example, a retired carpenter may be very happy to work with the younger children on special projects.

REACHING OUT TO YOUR COMMUNITY

Visit a retirement home. Bring flowers and appropriate wholesome snacks. Have the children help distribute them. Take special time to talk to the people; they will be especially interested in talking with the children.

REACHING OUT TO THE FORGOTTEN PEOPLE

Those in prison are truly the forgotten people. They are lonely and generally feel deserted. Many receive no visitors or letters. Some return to prison after their release, being unable to adjust to going back to a society they no longer feel a part of.

Arrange to write to and visit a prisoner. The children can write to the prisoner and in many states after proper clearances the whole family can visit him or her.

Check with your church to see what programs are available to you in your area. A good program will provide a screening process of both the prisoner and the potential friend.

HOME PRAYER TIME

Jesus answered them, "Remember this! If you have faith in God, you can say to this hill, 'Get up and throw yourself into the sea!' If you do not doubt in your heart, but believe that what you say will happen, it will be done for you. For this reason, I tell you: when you pray and ask for something, believe that you have received it, and you will be given whatever you ask for." Mark 11:22-24

What a fantastic idea! If I really, really believe my prayers will be answered it will happen? There have been times when I have needed guidance, not knowing which way my life was going. There have been times when I have prayed for others—in their sickness, their joys, their griefs. It seems that when I pray for people I have the confidence to believe that my prayers will be answered. It is not that I do not believe that what I pray for will come true. It is not that I do not believe what Christ said, it is just that my faith is not to the point of moving mountains—yet.

When I pray I know that the hills in my life will not fall into the sea. If they did, my immediate reaction would probably be disbelief. I pray for money and I think God just does not understand how impatient I am to have all that wealth. Or maybe I am blind to just how well off I really am.

There are times, however, when I know God has answered my prayers. These are the times when I have asked for strength to get through a difficult time in my life, a time when my world was in such a sorry shape I felt like running away.

The point I am making is that I have not given up on prayer as a strong and powerful force in my life, even though I may not have always felt my prayers were answered in the way I wanted. I need to continue to try to set my doubts aside and to deepen my belief in Christ and what he promised.

How does a family go about improving its prayer life? One way is to ask one another to share the different prayer experiences they have had. Experiment, try new approaches. And pray together, as a family, and with others.

FAMILY CANDLE PROJECT

In preparation for the prayer service that follows, your family might like to decorate a special Easter candle. This project could be scheduled a day ahead and the candle used throughout Lent and on Easter Sunday.

Materials:

Thick white or yellow candle, 6" tall
White tissue paper
Suggested symbols (See page 22)
Thin white glue
Permanent marking pens
5 whole cloves

Directions:

1. Choose some symbols suggested on the following page or your own designs.
2. Trace them onto tissue with permanent marking pens and carefully cut around the design.
3. Doing a small section at a time, brush glue onto the candle.
4. Flatten tissue cut-outs onto the candle.
5. With a heated ice pick make five holes in the side of candle, to form a cross.   Insert five whole cloves into the holes. Place the symbols Alpha A (the beginning) and Omega Ω (the end) above and below the cross.
6. Place flower bands around the top and bottom of the candle symbolizing everlasting life.

End the project with this reading:

Jesus answered, "The light will be among you a little longer. Continue on your way while you have the light, so the darkness will not come upon you; because the one who walks in the dark does not know where he is going. Believe in the light, then, while you have it, so that you will be people of the light."
John 12:35-36 (GNB)

EVENING PRAYER SERVICE

Start with a brief meditation. Light the candle and place it where it can be seen easily by everyone. Turn out the lights and let the flame become the center of focus. This will help keep out distractions. Allow everyone to become quiet within and remember that God is truly with us, *I am the light of the world.* (John 8:12) The length of the meditation should be geared to the age level of the children. For young children, a minute will seem like a very long time.

Choose some Bible passages that are favorites or might be fitting to your particular circumstances.

Some suggestions are:
For families with young children:

	Psalms 4:2
	Proverbs 23:15-16
	28:1
	Matthew 19:13-15
	Luke 9:46-48
	Acts 9:1-6
Husband and wife:	Song of Songs 2:1-7
	John 4:7-21
Adults and teens:	Ecclesiastes 3:1-8
	Psalms 22:1-12
	Proverbs 3
	Isaiah 42:1-4
	55:6-9
	Matthew 5:1-12
	Luke 10:25-37
	John 15:1-17

While everyone is still concentrated on the flame of the candle, (or some may prefer to close their eyes), the reader may read slowly the Biblical passage you have chosen and in a way that conveys as much meaning as possible. Try to concentrate on the feelings and images the reading inspires within you. If a thought or image distracts you and makes your mind wander, see where it takes you. If a particular phrase jumps out at you, remember it and study it—try to figure out its significance.

When the reading has been completed, allow a silence of a minute or two and share with one another your experiences. Let others reflect on your comments and compare them to their own. After everyone has had an opportunity to share, read through the passage a second time. Read slowly and with meaning. Generally, during the second reading, new thoughts and impressions surface. At the end of the reading, again, allow a reflection time and ask the family to share any new insights they may have.

Close each prayer session with a spontaneous prayer allowing everyone to participate, or use this closing prayer:

Lord, our family has just spent this time together with you.
We tried, Lord, to allow you to come to each of us in a unique and special way.
We took time to listen to you Lord;
To some of us, you seemed quiet,
To others, you spoke in a very clear and positive way.
Whatever the experience, Lord, help us to remember that you are with us always,
Remind us to continue to ask you for help and to give thanks and praise for all that is important to us in our lives.
And because we try to do good, we believe it pleases you, Lord.   Amen.

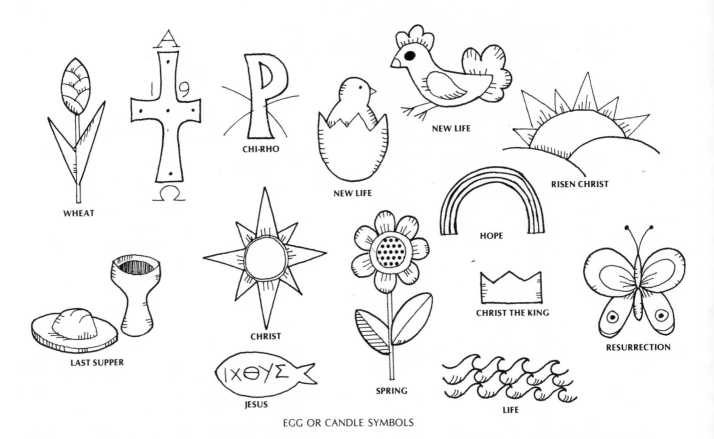

WHEAT

CHI-RHO

NEW LIFE

NEW LIFE

RISEN CHRIST

HOPE

CHRIST THE KING

RESURRECTION

LAST SUPPER

CHRIST

SPRING

LIFE

JESUS

EGG OR CANDLE SYMBOLS

CLEANING DAYS AT HOME

"Eek," was clearly heard throughout the house. The young girl leaped back as a large spider, discovered while he was in an apparent time of repose, dashed out from behind a picture. As he dived for a new hiding place, the girl, in a mild state of panic, ran to alert the rest of the family. Mother and the boys came running into the living room and nearly collided with the surprised girl. "What is it, Mary?" the Mother asked. "A giant spider," Mary gasped. "It nearly scared me to death!" Mother sighed and shook her head. "It all comes from neglect of the chores. Outside friends invite themselves in, get settled and make themselves at home and unless we ask them to leave, they'll stay on indefinitely." The boys laughed. The younger one, freckle-faced and wearing shiny braces, said, "Well, you're not going to trick me into doing any chores. I like spiders." Mother sighed again. "Easter will be here soon and we've got to get this house into some semblance of order. Besides, during the week before Easter it's the custom all over the world to clean house in preparation for the newness of the season. Do you remember the time we rented a cabin in the country?" The children nodded. "And do you remember when we got there the place was dusty and messy?" Again the heads nodded. "And what did we do?" Mom answered the question herself. "Of course, we cleaned up. We made the little cabin fit to live in. We must do the same here. We need to prepare our home, to renew and refresh our surroundings so we can feel refreshed and enthusiastic about being here. It's the same thing before we go on a trip. We clean house, and when we come home all is clean and our spirits are high and we are ready to begin again. And so we must clean our home now." "But," the older boy wrinkled his nose and said, "I hate to clean." Mother folded her arms. Then her face lit up. "All right, I have an idea! Since we all like games, I want you to try to think of a game that will make our cleaning more bearable." They hesitated for a few seconds, looked at one another quizzically, then slowly sauntered off to another part of the house.

When they returned, here is the game they devised: Using a compass and an 8½" x 11" sheet of lightweight cardboard, draw a circle 8" in diameter. Mark off into pie-shaped wedges. In each wedge write a chore to be done. Cut out and decorate. Cut out a spinner arrow. Punch a hole through the center of circle and spinner. Attach together loosely with a brad.

A CHILD'S HOUSECLEANING PRAYER

Dusting and cleaning, mopping and scrubbing . . .
Dear Lord, how difficult a task this is for me!
I would just as soon leave it all to someone else.
Or better yet why couldn't I wave a magic wand and have it all done! Poof!
Oh Lord, did you have to do all this kind of cleaning?
I can think of so many other things that I'd rather be doing. Important things too!
Please help me to do my chores.   Amen.

Lent—The Time of Drawing Closer

PALM SUNDAY

Palm Sunday begins the many traditions of Holy Week in churches throughout the world. For the first time the passion and death of Jesus is read from the Scriptures and people enter the solemn mood of the passing of their Lord. But before these words of suffering are heard, the Church invites us to celebrate a short-lived but glorious moment in the life of Jesus. It is his entrance into the city of Jerusalem.

It was the custom in those times that any leader or official was met at the gates of the city and escorted into town with people cheering along the way, waving palm branches and placing them on the dusty road to make a soft pathway for the person entering. The officials rode on donkeys or horses so all the people could see and follow them.

And so it happened that Jesus, when he arrived at the gates of Jerusalem that Sunday, was greeted by a throng of people who cheered him, waved palms, laid branches in his pathway, and followed after him singing. "Hosannah. Blessed is he who comes in the name of the Lord."

We celebrate that same glorious entrance by using palms and forming some kind of procession around our churches on Palm Sunday. It is our chance to give special praise to Jesus. Our palms are blessed, handed out to everyone, and after the ceremony it is the custom to take the palms home and display them in our houses in some way. Here are some ways your family might choose to display or use the palms you receive:

WOVEN PALM OR PAPER BASKET

A simple but attractive woven basket can be made using palm or construction paper strips. First assemble for each basket:

4 strips 1" x 17" for base
5 strips 1" x 18" for weaving
2 strips 2" x 18" for rim and handle
(for palm basket use longest palms for weaving, rim and handle, shortest palms for base)
stapler
scissors

Begin by shaping the four 1" x 17" strips into two crosses (a) and staple them together. Next place the two crosses together (b) and staple.

Now fold and crease the two strips of 2" x 18" paper in half *lengthwise* to form strips 1" x 18". Taking one of these strips form a loop and staple closed. This will be the rim. Next insert the eight strips (b) into the rim, adjust evenly and staple (c).

Starting at the rim begin weaving, over and under, the five 1" x 18" strips, being sure to adjust length and trim ends as you finish each piece. Staple each piece as you go (d).

Finish off by adding handle. Paper strips may be all one color or multi-colored.

Add some grass and eggs, and this sturdy handmade basket is ready to be given on Easter Sunday to a friend, neighbor or shut-in.

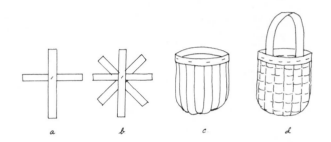

TENEBRAE—Celebrating Wednesday of Holy Week

The word "tenebrae" means darkness, and often on the Wednesday of Holy Week Christians commemorate Jesus' time of darkness in a special way. They want to feel and experience the loneliness that darkness can bring, the sensation of something ending, the sorrow that Jesus felt when his friends denied him or went off to sleep, one by one. Your family might also want to observe this time of darkness.

Place fifteen lighted candles in a row before your family. These candles should provide the only light in the room, so turn off all the lamps. Take a minute to notice how the fire dances on the candle, how the flame flickers, and how the shadows are in motion on the walls of the room.

Each member of the family reads a portion of Psalm 51, the Church's penitential song, and then blows out one of the candles. Continue to do this until all the candles but one are out.

1 Have mercy on me, O God, according to your loving kindness; in your great compassion blot out my offenses. (reader now blows out first candle)

2 Wash me through and through from my wicked-ness and cleanse me from my sin. For I know my transgressions, and my sin is ever before me.

3 Against you only have I sinned and done what is evil in your sight. And so you are justified when you speak and upright in your judgment.

4 Indeed, I have been wicked from my birth, a sinner from my mother's womb. For behold, you look for truth deep within me, and will make me understand wisdom secretly.

5 Purge me from my sin, and I shall be pure; wash me, and I shall be clean indeed. Make me hear of joy and gladness, that the body you have broken may rejoice. Hide your face from my sins and blot out all my iniquities.

6 Create in me a clean heart, O God, and renew a right spirit within me. Cast me not away from your presence and take not your holy Spirit from me.

7 Give me the joy of your saving help again and sustain me with your bountiful Spirit.

8 I shall teach your ways to the wicked, and sinners shall return to you.

9 Deliver me from death, O God, and my tongue shall sing of your righteousness, O God of my salvation.

10 Open my lips, O Lord, and my mouth shall pro-claim your praise.

11 Had you desired it, I would have offered sacrifice, but you take no delight in burnt offerings.

12 The sacrifice of God is a troubled spirit; a broken and contrite heart, O God, you will not despise.

13 Be favorable and gracious to Zion, and rebuild the walls of Jerusalem.

14 Then you will be pleased with the appointed sacrifices, with burnt offerings and oblations; then shall they offer young bullocks upon your altar.

Everyone says together the Doxology

15 Glory be to the Father, and to the Son, and to the Holy Spirit; as in the beginning, it is now, and ever shall be, world without end. Amen. (blow out the last candle)

Remain silent for a few minutes in the darkness and then invite each family member to offer a prayer for true understanding of the suffering of God's people.

A LAST SUPPER AT HOME

PART I

Have you ever wondered what kind of meal Christ shared with his apostles at the Last Supper? Did he put new meaning into an ordinary meal or did he change a meal that was already something special to them all? Well, it seems that it probably was a very special event. The Gospels all set the time during the Jewish feast of Passover. Maybe some members of the family can find the Gospel passages that refer to the Last Supper and set the time of year (spring).

Read: Matthew 26:1-35
       Mark 14:1-31
       Luke 22:1-38

Just what was the Passover meal? What was it like? Why was and is it still important to the Jewish people?

Read: Exodus 12:1-28

We have celebrations such as our own Thanksgiving holiday, that are similar to the Passover. If the Passover event and the flight into the desert marked the beginning of the search for the Promised Land and the beginning of a homeland for the Hebrew people, could it not also be a thanksgiving celebration? How do you celebrate your own Thanksgiving meal? Do you follow certain rituals and menus almost every year? What of our own American history. We also had a flight (from Europe), and a search for religious freedom in our background. Can you envision how you might feel if Christ were to be with your family at a Thanksgiving dinner and have him change it to make it very special to you?

Are there other times when we experience "Last Suppers" in our lives? Times such as an older son or daughter leaving home to go to college? Or the times we have family reunions when relatives visit from all over. Days are spent putting together the meal with many people adding their "specialties" to the menu. There are greetings, laughter and memories—memories of the last reunion, and Uncle Max who died last December and how much he enjoyed seeing all the family together. It was Uncle Max's "Last Supper" and in a way he is still with us as we remember him. That kind of meal is truly more than just another dinner with the family. If your family has talked about these kinds of suppers and wants to participate during the

Lenten season in a special Passover service, the following is presented for your use.

PART II

The Passover ceremony given here is considerably different than that of the Jewish tradition. It has been shortened and adapted for a wide variety of families.

All the roles may be shared by several people, and families are encouraged to do so. This is especially applicable if more than one family has gathered together for this celebration.

NARRATOR(S): Explain(s) the ceremonial blessings and the significance of each part of the meal. To assure smoothness throughout the ceremony the narrator(s) should have read over the parts and know the sequence well.
COMMENTATOR(S): These roles can be for older members of the family.
READERS: These can be the roles of the children.

On the table are several unlit candles.

You will need 3 plates:

one with  one with one with

and a pitcher of grape juice to be placed in front of the commentators who will bless these foods.

Each person should have a glass and a plate with a piece of celery, some Haroses salad and a bit of horseradish (or a radish).

A cup of salt water can be shared by every four people.

Have a Bible with assigned passages marked.

Assign roles.

The various foods represent the following:

Haroses salad
—slavery, the making of bricks to build the Pharaoh's pyramids

Matzo
—the unleavened bread of affliction

Horseradish
—bitter herbs, the suffering of slavery

Celery
—green spring plants

Salt water
—tears

Meat
—pascal lamb

LAST SUPPER SERVICE

NARRATOR: My friends, we are gathered this evening to commemorate two great feasts in the history of mankind—the Jewish Passover and the Last Supper. The Jewish Passover is a remembrance of the liberation of Egypt. The Egyptians forced the sons of Israel into slavery. God told his people he would strike down all the first-born of Egypt. In their marked houses the Hebrews would be safe from Yahweh's destroying plague. He would "pass over" them. The Hebrews hurriedly departed from the land of Egypt with their bread, still unrisen, on their shoulders. Through Moses, God brought them out of slavery. In remembrance of this they honored God with rituals and feasting. It was and still is a thanksgiving meal. It is a meal accompanied by stories, prayers, chants and blessings. It is a meal which can be meaningful to us all. We can relate the symbolism of this meal to the struggles in our own history against the bondage of slavery and the thirst for freedom.

On the last day of his life Jesus took part in this festival meal with his disciples. It was during this Last Supper that he gave us his body and blood with the invitation "Take and eat— drink of it, all of you." He gave us a meal which is a thanksgiving. The Greek word for thanksgiving is "Eucharist." Tonight we will celebrate together a simple adaption of the Jewish Passover meal in order to understand better and appreciate the significance of that meal and our own Christian meal, often called the Eucharist, which originates from it.

Let us begin by lighting the candles before us.
_____ will recite the blessing over them.

COMMENTATOR: Blessed are you, Lord God, King of the Universe, who has made us holy with your commandments. As we light these candles help us to remember to live according to your word so that we may bring the light to others.
NARRATOR: We will now hear an explanation of the symbols of the traditional Passover meal.
READER: This is the **matzo**—the unleavened bread which reminds us of how the Hebrew people left Egypt in a hurry and did not have time to prepare for the trip.
READER: These **bitter herbs** of horseradish recall to us the pain and suffering of slavery.

READER: This is **celery**—a green spring plant. Passover is a spring feast. A reminder to us of the newness of life.

READER: This **salt water** is like the tears of a people who are bound up in slavery and are not free.

READER: The **haroses salad**—a mixture of fruit, nuts, honey and wine helps us remember the labors of slavery and the making of mortar and bricks.

NARRATOR: Let us now listen to the questions so we may further understand the symbolism of this meal.

ALL: Why do we eat matzo or unleavened bread?

READER: The Hebrews left Egypt in a hurry. Their dough did not have time to rise.

ALL: Why do we eat bitter herbs?

READER: We eat bitter herbs to remind us of the bitterness of slavery.

ALL: Why do we dip twice?

READER: The first time we dip celery into salt water to show that we believe in freedom. The second time we dip horseradish into haroses salad to show that the bitterness of slavery has been sweetened.

ALL: What is the meaning of Pesach?

READER: Pesach means the pascal lamb which the Hebrews sacrificed to God in remembrance of the night the Holy One passed over their houses.

NARRATOR: _____ will now bless the grape juice.

COMMENTATOR: Blessed are you, Lord God, King of the Universe, Creator of the fruit of the vine.

NARRATOR: The juice is poured from a common vessel symbolizing our unity. All may now drink.

(pause)

_____ now blesses the green spring vegetable, the celery.

COMMENTATOR: Blessed are you, Lord God, King of the Universe, Creator of the fruit of the earth and all growing things. Keep us ever mindful of the bounties of our lands, and aware of the needs of others.

NARRATOR: Everyone dips the celery into salt water and eats of it.

(pause)

_____ will now break the matzo in two. He will put half of it on the dish and put the other half aside for later. It was probably this second half that Christ took and blessed after the Last Supper.

COMMENTATOR: _(lifts plate of matzo for all to see)_ This is the bread of affliction which our forefathers ate. All who are hungry—let them come and eat. All who are thirsty—let them come and drink. All who are needy —let them come and celebrate this meal with us. Keep us ever mindful of the needs of our brothers and sisters—for those who hunger for knowledge and truth and your word, O Lord.

NARRATOR: As _____ blesses, breaks and passes the matzo, we are reminded, as with the juice shared from a common vessel, that the sharing of a single matzo indicates unity. "Because there is one bread, all of us, though many, are one body, because we share the same loaf" (1 Cor. 10:17).

COMMENTATOR: Blessed are you, Lord God, King of the Universe, who brings forth bread from the earth. You nourish us both in body and spirit.

NARRATOR: _____ breaks the matzo into small pieces. While it is being passed let us pray together:

ALL: Blessed are you, Lord God, King of the Universe, who made us holy with your commandments and directed us concerning the eating of matzo.

(pause while all eat matzo)

NARRATOR: Now everyone dips horseradish into haroses salad and says:

ALL: Blessed are you, Lord God, King of the Universe, who made us holy with your commandments and directed us concerning the eating of bitter herbs. Keep us ever mindful of the gifts of freedom, liberty and justice.

NARRATOR: All make a sandwich of matzo, horseradish and salad and eat.

(pause, break and pass more matzo)

NARRATOR: _____ will now bless the lamb.

COMMENTATOR: Blessed are you, Lord God, King of the Universe, Creator of all living things. Let this lamb help to remind us of our brothers and sisters everywhere who go hungry.

The festival meal may now be served. Let us share this meal in joy, remembering that Christ is with us.

ALL: Christ is with us.   AMEN.

Note: It would be appropriate at the end of this meal to read Matthew's account of the Last Supper 26:26-29 and again to share the matzo.

MENU

Lamb Stew or Roast Leg of Lamb
Rice Pilaf
Raw Vegetable Plate
Haroses Salad
Matzo
Pound Cake for Dessert (optional)

Lamb Stew

2 lb. lamb cut into 2"
    cubes
1 onion, chopped
4 cups hot broth
4 carrots, diced
1 small turnip, diced
2 cups potatoes, cubed
2 teaspoons salt
¼ teaspoon pepper
1 bay leaf
½ pkg. frozen peas,
    thawed

Directions:

Brown meat and onion well in hot fat. Drain. Add broth. Simmer, covered, for 2 hours. Add remaining ingredients. Continue cooking until vegetables are tender, about ½ hour. Broth may be thickened with ¼ cup flour mixed with ½ cup cold water. Serves 6.

Haroses Salad

6 tart apples, peeled,
    cored and chopped
½ cup chopped walnuts
½ teaspoon cinnamon
2 Tablespoons honey
¼ cup sweet red wine
Mix well. Serves 6.

Note: Reserve part of this amount, about 1 tsp per person to be used during service. The rest to be eaten at festival meal.

Rice Pilaf

1¼ cups raw long grain rice
½ cube butter
2 cups boiling water
1 chicken bouillon cube
salt and pepper

Directions:

In a large heavy skillet saute rice in butter until golden brown. Remove from heat and add water and bouillon. Cover with tight-fitting lid and simmer slowly for 30 to 45 minutes or until liquid is absorbed and rice is tender. Place in buttered casserole. Put in 300° oven for 30 minutes. Serves 6.

To serve 12:

2½ cups rice
4 cups hot water
2 bouillon cubes

THE WASHING OF FEET

Who washes your feet? We don't usually go around washing each other's feet. It is not necessary—they get washed every time we take a shower! However, two thousand years ago when Christ lived, the washing of feet was very important.

Try to picture how it was then. Only the main highways were paved in stone to allow movement of the Roman armies. The roads and streets were very dusty when they were dry, and when they were wet, a mud bath. People either walked barefoot or in sandals. Can you imagine trying to keep your house clean with everyone coming in with feet covered with dust or mud? Well, the people who could afford it had slaves to wash the feet of the guests of the house. Those who could not afford slaves probably did not care anyway because they had dirt floors.

The devil had already induced Judas, son of Simon Iscariot to hand him over; and so during the supper, Jesus—fully aware that he had come from God and was going to God, the Father who had handed everything over to him—rose from the meal and took off his cloak. He picked up a towel and tied it around himself. Then he poured water into a basin and began to wash his disciples' feet and dry them with the towel he had around him. Thus he came to Simon Peter, who said to him "Lord, are you going to wash my feet?" Jesus answered, "You may not realize now what I am doing, but later you will understand." Peter replied, "You shall never wash my feet!" "If I do not wash you," Jesus answered, "You will have no share in my heritage." "Lord," Simon Peter said to him, "then not only my feet, but my hands and head as well." Jesus told him, "The man who has bathed has no need to wash (except for his feet); he is entirely cleansed, just as you are; though not all." (The reason he said, "Not all are washed clean." was that he knew his betrayer.)

After he had washed their feet, he put his cloak back on and reclined at the table once more. He said to them:

"Do you understand what I just did for you? You address me as 'Teacher' and 'Lord,' and fittingly enough for that is what I am. But if I washed your feet—I who am Teacher and Lord—then you must wash each other's feet. What I just did was to give you an example: as I have done, so you must do. I solemnly assure you, no slave is greater than his master; no messenger outranks the one who sent him. Once you know all these things, blest will you be if you put them into practice."

John 13:2-17 (TNAB)

What lesson did Jesus teach to the disciples by washing their feet?

Why not try it and see what we can learn about what it all means firsthand.

A TOWEL PROJECT

Let us start by each preparing our own towel for the rite of washing of feet of the family. Family members can personalize their own towels with symbols, words or names of their own choosing. Use long strips of paper towels or some inexpensive dish towel material. The decorations can remain a surprise until you come together for the rite. It would be wise to plan this project at least a day ahead of the washing ritual.

FAMILY WASHING RITE

Gather the family together and sit in a circle. Place a pan or basin one quarter full of water in the center. Soap is not necessary but a few drops of bath oil might be a nice touch. Provide a washcloth or sponge for washing and bring the towels you have made beforehand.

Start by reading John 13:2-17.

Use some appropriate background music.

Ask everyone to be particularly aware of his or her feelings as they wash each other's feet.

Then take some time to allow everyone to talk about what it felt like.

Which did they like most, to wash or be washed? Why?

Concluding reading: Luke 7:36-50.

THE DEATH OF JESUS

There is not one of us who has not been touched in some way by death. Whether it is the passing of a loved one or a casual friend, we have all experienced some of the emptiness and grief that inevitably accompanies death. And we all have different ways of grieving. Counselors offer ways of helping us and others during these difficult times. But in the end, there will be a time when the family, all alone, must comfort and support one another.

One may wonder how Jesus' family felt after his death. Of course they must have been deeply saddened by his death, but were they also angry at those who killed him? Did they think there was something they could have said or done to change matters? How did they feel about those who denied and deserted Jesus? Were they resentful or forgiving? How did they mourn and comfort one another? Were they fearful that they too might be persecuted?

Perhaps your family would like to replay the scene of the burial of Jesus in modern context.

1. As if Jesus had been living with your family, choose a gathering place that would have been his favorite (the garden, a place at table, an armchair before the fireplace).

2. Choose a Scripture passage, one of the stories Jesus told, which might have been his favorite and read it aloud.

3. Have each family member take turns telling part of the story of how Jesus was taken to his death. For example, someone may start by saying, "Jesus returned from praying. His friend Judas approached him accompanied by many men armed with swords and clubs. One of Jesus' friends pulled out his sword and. . . ." The next person relates, in his own words, what happens next. Each person takes a turn telling the story until at last all have spoken and the story is complete.

4. Play an appropriate record as you think about the meaning of his death.

5. Have each family member be one of Jesus' friends (Peter, Mary, the weeping woman, Mary Magdalene, John, et al) and talk about how you feel at the death and burial of your Lord. For instance, Peter might say, "I feel so badly that I denied him. Three times I denied he was my friend. I wish I could take the words back." Mary might say, "I am weak with grief. My heart has endured so much. I think it will break. I feel afraid and lonely now that he is gone."

6. Light a candle (or several) and close with this prayer:

God, Our Father, as surely as we grieve the death of loved ones,
Just as confident we are that you shall give them light.
This light is the new life of the risen Jesus who takes away our tears and becomes ever more present.
Be with us in our pain, our separation, and our grief.
Give us the consolation of each other's love.
Through Jesus who died and rose again.   Amen.

FURTHER CHOICES

Read the burial of Jesus (Matthew 27:57-66) and discuss the following options on how to meditate further and consider the burial of Jesus.

1. Ask each member to plan his own burial service. (Sample service planned by a twelve-year-old boy might be:

"I would like to have my family and friends attend. Also my teachers and other relatives should be invited. The music could be from *Godspell* or *The Sting*. Read the story of Lazarus. Have a slide show of "Me and My Pet." Be sure to keep it simple and have something to eat.")

2. If children are too young or this is too difficult a task, suggest they plan a service for one of their pets.

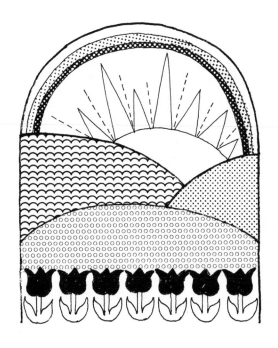

Easter

We snuggle together, our family
to keep warm in these early hours of Easter,
to hear the great announcement:
    Christ is risen!

        We snuggle together—mother, father, children
            to hug,
            to embrace,
            to share Peace-that-passes-understanding,
            to delight in open hearts and glad spirits!

                In the touching
                    we find each other changed,
                    more hopeful,
                    cleansed from the ghosts of the past,
                    more of a family.
                        Why?
                        We ask every year, why?
                        We're not sure. They say, "Christ is risen!"
                    We know only that this is mystery,
                        and our whole world is changed because of it.
                        Only God really knows the hows and the whys.
                            But we know the celebration,
                                the delight,
                                the hope.

Easter—Customs Around the World

EGGS

The egg, as an ancient symbol of fertility, is older than Christianity itself. It reaches far beyond any one religion. Throughout history this symbol has had significant meaning for mankind. With the birth of Christianity, it took on a new symbolism, that of resurrection and the miracle of new life. The chick (new life) lies unborn in the egg (the tomb), only to break forth in triumphant new life!

As far back as the Egyptian, Persian, and Greek civilizations eggs were colored, decorated and even given as gifts. Coloring suggested joy and the longing for the profusion of colors spring can bring. People still enjoy the art of decorating and giving eggs at Easter time. Russians and Ukranians are noted for their handsomely decorated eggs called *pysanky*, which means "to write." These eggs are covered with unique designs and are very colorful. In these countries, as well as in Poland and Czechoslovakia, baskets of eggs and other food items are blessed at church on Holy Saturday to be used for the Easter morning's breakfast. The giving of eggs is also practiced in Holland where Dutch children go from house to house on Palm Sunday singing and asking for colored eggs.

The custom of egg rolling originated in England based on the idea of the great stone being rolled away from Christ's tomb. British settlers brought this custom to the new world and to this day hard-boiled eggs are still rolled on the White House lawn in Washington, D.C. by enthusiastic children on Easter Monday.

Easter colors

White—light, purity, joy
Yellow—sunlight, radiance
Purple—royalty, mourning
Green—nature, hope of eternal life
Red—Joy of Easter

Egg-Coloring Projects

BATIK EGGS (Pysanky-type design)

Materials:

hard-boiled eggs
dye solution—yellow, red, purple
yellow crayon, sharpened
paper toweling

Directions:

For best results use warm, dry hard-boiled eggs. (Warm ones will take the wax crayon better). Use a sharp pointed *yellow* crayon to draw your designs. When coloring, start with lighter color dye and progress to darker color. Eggs absorb dye quickly. Start again with fresh dye if colors begin to fade. Read all directions thoroughly.

Begin by drawing either symmetrical or symbolic designs on the egg with a sharp crayon. Wax crayon will resist the dye so all areas under these drawings will remain **white** when dyed.

Dip egg in hot **yellow** dye. Blot dry with a paper towel.

Now crayon in the next areas of design over the dyed area. (These areas will remain yellow when dipped in the next color.)

Now dip the egg in hot **red** dye. Blot dry.

Next crayon in some final details of your design. (These areas will remain red when dipped in the next color and all areas not waxed-in will be purple.)

Lastly, dip egg in **purple** dye. Blot dry.

Have fun experimenting with designs and colors.

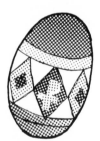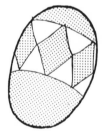

NATURE EGGS

Materials:

Old nylon stockings
Plastic bag ties
Dye solution
Paper toweling
Small leaves and foilage such as geranium, Japanese maple, carrot tops, parsley, etc.
Hard-boiled eggs

Directions:

Cut a 5″ square piece of old nylon stocking for each egg.

Place a small leaf in the middle of the square of nylon. Place egg over leaf and gently stretch nylon around egg and fasten with a plastic tie.

Dip into dye until desired color is reached. Remove. Pat lightly with paper towel. Let dry slightly before unwrapping.

DYE SOLUTIONS

Ordinary food coloring works quite successfully for coloring eggs. Place several drops in a cup. Add 1 teaspoon white vinegar. Fill cup with boiling water.

Or:

Try boiling walnut shells or leftover coffee grounds in a small amount of water for a brown color. Strain and add a teaspoon of white vinegar to set color. Skins from yellow onions produce a lovely shade of yellow.

EASTER PARADES

In many cities and countries, the Easter Parade brings out an array of bright new clothes and bonnets. The origin of this custom comes from a belief that if one wore new clothes on Easter morning, the year would be one of good luck.

Christians have adapted the custom to mean that new clothes on Easter Sunday signify new life and a fresh start. If your family wishes to participate in some form of this custom, here are suggestions:

—Ahead of time, decide that each person will have *one* new piece of clothing, whether it is shoes, or a dress, or socks, or even a new handkerchief. The important thing is that it is agreed upon ahead of time.

—The night before Easter or some time early in the morning, have each person appear carrying the piece of clothing. Use this prayer of blessing:

God our Father and Creator, it is you who give us all good gifts, and you who bring us the sense of joy and freshness at something new. Bless these clothes of ours that are new. We wear them in joy and with a feeling of celebration at the resurrection of your son. Help us always to remember those who have less than we do, those who need our sharing and our love, through Christ Our Lord. Amen.

(You might also suggest during Lent that each member of the family work on making some new item of clothing to wear on Easter morning.)

—Make Easter morning a time of taking family pictures with each member in his or her new clothes.

—Invite friends and relatives to an Easter Walk around your neighborhood or to a park or church for your very own parade.

—Suggest that each person in your family find some flower to wear as a decoration in buttonholes, in the hair, etc., for Easter morning as a sign of the celebration of new life.

SUNRISE AT EASTER

If you live near Mount Holyoke, the Hollywood Bowl, Mount Davidson in San Francisco, Pikes Peak or near any large city or natural park in our country, then perhaps you have experienced the Easter morning sunrise service.

Thousands of persons on that one morning of the year arrive while it is still dark to attend the ecumenical services of song, prayer, sermon and silence while watching the sun rise and proclaiming that Jesus is again alive.

If you do not live near one of these areas but would like to greet the sun or create a kind of service of your own, here are some suggestions:

—Search out, several days in advance, a natural setting where the sun can be clearly seen as it rises. Find out the time of the sunrise and invite people to arrive a half hour in advance.

—Choose some appropriate songs to sing as you sit in the semi-darkness awaiting the rising sun, for example, *Have You Seen Jesus My Lord?* or *Praise Him in the Morning*, or *Kumbaya*.

—As the time grows closer for the sun to rise, you might want to act out the scene of the women who went to the tomb to anoint the body of Jesus on the first Easter:

WOMAN 1: Here it is, the same tomb, but something is changed. The stone is moved. Perhaps someone is already here to anoint the body of the Lord.

WOMAN 2: Beloved he was. We bring our oils and perfumes and touch the body of the Lord.

WOMAN 3: But there is no body, there is nothing! He is gone! The body has been stolen!

(The three women sink down to their knees and begin to cry, covering their faces. Two persons, messengers — angels — come forward)

MESSENGER: You are looking for Jesus. Why do you search for him here? He is not here. He is among the living. Go search for him among the people.

MESSENGER 2: He is not here. He has been raised up. Remember what he said to you while he was still in Galilee—that the Son of Man must be delivered into the hands of sinful men, and be crucified, and on the third day rise again.

(The three women turn towards the place where the sun is to rise and walk towards it)

—A song to listen to, especially if you are in a setting where a record or cassette player could be used, is the section from Handel's *Messiah* "I Know That My Redeemer Liveth." Or, choose a favorite Easter Song for all to sing, here is an example:

Jesus Christ is risen today, alleluia!
Our triumphant holy day, alleluia!
Who did once upon the cross, alleluia!
Suffer to redeem our loss, alleluia!

Hymns of praise then let us sing, alleluia!
Unto Christ, our heav'nly King, alleluia!
Who endured the cross and grave, alleluia!
Sinners to redeem and save, alleluia!

— Include some prayers either from the Easter liturgy of your church or ones you have written yourself to give thanks to the risen Jesus. You may want to begin some prayers that all can share with the words:

Jesus, today I thank you especially because. . . .

or

Jesus, I see you this day in my life as. . . .

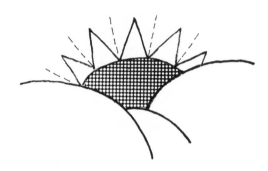

HATS, CLOTHES, AND COSTUMES

Children often grumble and resist Mom or Dad's attempt to take them shopping for new clothes. They may say, "Why do we need new things? I hate to shop." Another may respond to the idea of a shopping trip enthusiastically and bright-eyed with, "I love to get new clothes!" A teenager might say, "I like shopping only if I can go by myself and pick out my own things."

For many families new outfits and Easter go hand in hand. Youngsters sometimes question this custom, as they would rather be outside practicing for an up-coming baseball or soccer game. On the other hand, others like to make a day out of clothes shopping, planning lunch out or a stop at a special ice cream parlor. Still others will placidly allow themselves to be dragged from store to store in quest of Easter finery. On such an excursion a child may reach the end of his or her rope and defiantly ask in a loud voice, "Why do we have to go through all this?" In an attempt to answer this question one discovers that there actually is logic associated with our present-day custom of fancy Easter clothes.

Historically, in many European countries the peasants wore layers of clothes throughout the cold winters. As spring and Easter approached, signifying a new beginning, heavier clothes were shed in favor of lighter ones. People saved their new things for Easter or washed their old ones to prepare themselves. Usually this change of clothes occurred during the week before

Easter as this was the time of most Christian Baptisms. White gowns, symbolizing purity, light, and joy, were worn by those fortunate to have them following the Baptismal ceremony. Thus White Week, later to be called Holy Week, was celebrated by many.

ACTIVITY: For many people in the world today there will be no new Easter bonnet much less an entire outfit. In order to heighten our awareness of those less fortunate than ourselves, try to get the children involved with the plight of the paper doll family.

Have the children trace the dolls and outfits on pages 33 and 34. Older children may assist the younger ones.

SET THE SCENE: Our story begins in a poor section of town. The family members have just begun their evening meal. Easter is two weeks away and they are discussing plans.

READ the following unfinished sentences for each doll and encourage the children to try to complete them.

Daughter: If we don't have new clothes, Easter won't . . .

Mother: Grandmother has been so sick . . . Medical expenses . . .

Son: I have a paper route; I can get my own outfit. I want . . .

Father: Clothes don't make the person. I think . . .

Grandmother: When I was a girl . . .

Grandfather: Oh, don't worry. Let's . . .

Baby: Da Da . . .

You might also ask:

What else might they say?

How will the family celebrate Easter even if they don't have new clothes?

If clothes were not all new, what could be added to brighten up the outfit?

In what other ways can we make our things new?

A PAPER DOLL PRAYER

Dear Lord, here is my paper doll family,
Their faces never change,
And their legs don't bend.
But Lord, I can make them laugh, cry, shout, or whisper.
I can make them go anywhere in the world.
They can live in a castle on the big living room couch,
Or be so poor, they have to have a cereal box for their house.
Thank you, Lord, for these very special friends.
They make me very happy.   Amen.

FATHER

MOTHER

SISTER

BABY

BROTHER

GRANDMOTHER

GRANDFATHER

33

Easter—The Hope of New Life

VERNAL EQUINOX

What is the vernal equinox and what does it have to do with Easter?

The word equinox is Latin and means equal nights. It represents one of two times during the year when day and nights are equally long. This occurs once early in the year at springtime and once toward the end of the year in the autumn.

Since earliest times the vernal equinox represented the start of the spring season and was celebrated with feasts and pageantry because this was the season for the harvesting of the winter crops of wheat, flax, and rye and the planting of the summer crops.

Now, many of us are city people and are no longer in touch with planting and harvesting of crops. Maybe we need to renew our acquaintance with the seasons and growing of crops. One way is to plant a family vegetable garden. Even people living in the heart of the city can plant a herb garden, using large clay pots or wooden planters.

A garden, whether in a pot or a plot, can act as a lasting symbol of spring and the Easter season. An Easter garden can act as a constant reminder of new beginnings.

PREPARE THE GARDEN

Begin by asking your family to tell what spring means to them—how they perceive the earth changing as the days become longer and warmer. You may want to discuss how mankind, from earliest times, believed that by carefully tilling the soil and caring for the crops and flocks, they were honoring God and hoped they would be rewarded for their labors.

May you be blessed in the city, and blessed in the country!

Blessed be the fruit of your womb, the produce of your soil and the offspring of your livestock, the issue of your herds and the young of your flocks!

Blessed be your grain bin and your kneading bowl!

May you be blessed in your coming in, and blessed in your going out!   Deuteronomy 28:3-6 (TNAB)

Plan what type of plants to grow, where you are going to plant them, and how to care for them. Have the children research which are the best crops to grow in your area. Local nurseries or 4-H chapters are good resources to use.

After the ground has been prepared and the seeds planted, say this prayer while the garden is being watered for the first time:

Lord God, Creator of heaven and earth, and of all living things,

Please bless this ground that has been so carefully and lovingly prepared.

Bless the seeds we have planted, that they will bring forth a plentiful crop.

Bless the sun and water you provide to us, so our crop can be nourished.

Bless our labor that we may continue to learn and grow through this experience.   Amen.

Why does Easter fall on a different day each year?

To answer this question an understanding of calendars is needed. Christ's passion, death, and resurrection coincided with the Jewish Passover feast (Matthew 26:1-2; Mark 14:1; Luke 22:1; John 11:55). Passover occurs in the spring on the 14th day of the Jewish month of Nisan. The Jewish calendar is based on a solar year of 365¼ days, like our own calendar, but has a lunar month of 29½ days. There are twelve lunar months which make up a year of only 364 days. So periodically a month (Adar) would be added at the end of the year to make the lunar year coincide with the solar year. The month of Adar was chosen to make sure that Passover would always occur after the vernal equinox.

The early Christian churches had a dispute among themselves as to when Easter should fall. The Jewish Christians felt it should always fall on Passover regardless of the day of the week. While the gentile Christians felt that Easter should always be observed on Sunday since that was the day of the week that the resurrection had occurred. For the first three hundred years after Christ's death Easter was celebrated at two different times, with the eastern churches generally following the Jewish tradition, while the western churches followed the Sunday tradition.

In 325 A.D., Constantine convened the Nicene Council and it was decided to have Easter fall on the first Sunday after the full moon following the vernal equinox. One exception was if the first Sunday also coincided with Passover, then Easter would fall on the second Sunday. Thus, Easter has remained a moveable holy day falling anywhere between March 22 and April 25.

A FAMILY CALENDAR

The calendar that you use in your home has much useful information besides the months, weeks, and days of the year. It will show all the important holidays, and if it is a church calendar, it will have the important liturgical events of the year.

However, each family also has its own special days; birthdays of family and friends, vacation times, first communions, confirmations, anniversaries are all examples of times we like to remember. Purchase next year's calendar and fill in all these important remembrances. Pick a special date to be your "family day" when you will celebrate being a family. Plan for your day as if it were an important holiday.

Keep your calendars from year to year and see how some dates will carry on while others will be dropped and new ones added.

ANIMALS—SYMBOLS OF NEW LIFE

Many of our familiar animals are in some way connected with or used as symbols for Easter. Easter Day or some free time during that season might be an appropriate time to search out these animals and study them, either in the zoo, in pet shops, or in their natural habitats. Here are the animals and the things they symbolize.

The OWL: Because an owl prefers darkness to light, it becomes a reminder to us at Easter that, like the owl, we sometimes choose the darkness of sin, but we await in our hearts the light of Jesus.

The ROBIN: The legend of the robin tells us that it plucked a thorn from the forehead of Christ, staining its breast red. Since that time all robins are red-breasted.

The LION: Ancient peoples believed that lion cubs were born dead and that when they were three days old the lioness breathed on them and brought them to life. Thus they became a symbol of the three days Christ lay dead in the tomb and then lived again.

The WHALE: Because of the story of Jonah, which many of the early Christians interpreted as a prophecy about Jesus, the whale became an Easter animal. As Jonah lay three days in the belly of the whale and then was cast upon dry land, so Jesus was raised from the darkness into the light after three days.

The BUTTERFLY is symbolic of the Easter cycle. In its first stage, as caterpillar, it represents life, then the cocoon signifies death, and finally the butterfly comes forth in new life.

The RABBIT is a symbol of fertility. It has long been used as an Easter pet to assure us of the growth of new life and the special gifts of Easter.

The EAGLE: The eagle is the only bird that can look directly at the light of the sun. It was often thought that the eagle flew so high that its feathers were scorched by the heat of the sun. Therefore, coming so close to death, the eagle was a bird of great nobility, a symbol of Christ.

The PEACOCK is a symbol of new life and Easter because each spring it renews its vibrant blue and green feathers.

The LAMB, because it was sacrificed in ancient times at Passover, was likened to Jesus who was sacrificed for us. Jesus is the Lamb of God as well as the Good Shepherd who protects us and invites us to refreshing waters. Often at Easter time the butter, cakes, or a jellied salad are formed into the shape of a lamb.

Besides a visit or a search for these animals and birds, members of the family might wish to take some Easter time to read further about them, to look for TV specials on them, or to make cards and share Easter messages using the symbols of the animals.

An old Spanish custom still prevails in Southern California where each year on Holy Saturday or during the Easter season children bring their pets to the local church to be blessed. The animals are groomed and decorated and everyone gathers together on the church patio for this special ceremony. The following blessing is used:

Almighty Father, we bless the animals for all they have done for us in supplying our food, in carrying our burdens, and in providing companionship and rendering service to mankind since the world began.

After the animals are blessed, white doves are released and Mexican musicians fill the air with their music.

Since spring and Easter time are days when new life and little animals are important, your family might want to observe the time with a discussion or project on respect for all living things. You might, for example:

— Take a walk in your neighborhood and watch for all the animals and birds that live there. Later, have everyone draw sketches of the animals and where they live.

— In your own yard with your pets and the neighborhood animals, birds, bugs, etc., give thanks to God with the prayer above.

Then have a treat for yourselves and the animals!

PLANTING, WAITING FOR NEW LIFE

Opa (Dutch for grandfather) once remarked that he found spiritual meaning in his plants and soil. Well versed in plant care, he not only could name nearly every plant in one's garden but could also correctly recite its genus name. He has said many times the greatest thrill for him is the planting, waiting, care, patient watching, and final triumph when new growth begins to erupt from the soil. He believed that when he was working with the soil he came closest to achieving inner peace. Moreover, he believed new growth was a constant reminder of the hope we need to have in each other.

In the spirit of Easter, perhaps your family would like to do a plant project.

ACTIVITY:

Prepare ahead:

seeds or bulbs native to your area
book on plant care
popsicle sticks
small cards — 3 x 5 will do
potting soil
pots

Plan:

Alone or with one or two other families begin by reading the parable of the sower (Matthew 13:1-9) or the mustard seed (Matthew 13:31-32).

Choose the seeds or bulbs you wish to plant.

Research the care, history, planting instructions and summarize on the card.

Plant the seeds, label the stick, and put it in the pot.

As a remembrance of this time, with the extra seeds you might try the following seed project:

FRIENDSHIP GARDEN

Invite a few families to gather for shared prayer during an evening of Lent. Ask each family to bring one or two packets of their favorite flower seeds or leftover seeds from the plant project.

At the end of the prayer time exchange the seeds so that each family has a variety of seeds to be planted in a Friendship Garden.

SEED CROSS

Materials:

a cross cut out of cardboard about 7" high
various seeds and pods such as:
  sunflower
  dried peas
  pinto, white, and lima beans
  lentils
  dried corn
  white glue

Glue the seeds and pods in a pleasing design onto the cross.

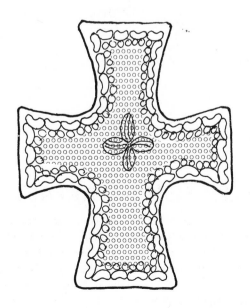

PLANT PRAYER

Our little seeds are in the soil now, Lord.
As you watch and care for us, so we will look after our plants.
When we love them we will see them sprout, showing us the smiles of their flowers and fine greenery.
These plants, Lord, help us to remember how beautiful your garden is!
Help us always to care for them.   Amen.

EASTER FISH BREAKFAST

When Jesus came back to life on Easter morning, to be with his family and friends again, he did ordinary kinds of things so they would believe and recognize him. We can imagine his yawning at the early hour of the day, putting on his sandals, and beginning to think about his breakfast. A warm fish breakfast would have tasted great, for most of Jesus' friends were fishermen.

One of the favorite Easter stories is that of Jesus on the shore of the Sea of Tiberias, cooking breakfast and calling out to his friends to bring their catch in and join him. Your family could relive that first Easter morning with such a special breakfast. Your menu could consist of fish and bread and something to drink; fish crackers, or biscuits cut into the shape of fish would be appropriate.

1. Before the meal begins, someone could read the story of that fish breakfast: John 21:1-14.
2. Then, someone could lead the rest of the family in a special Grace that fits the theme of the day —that everything, including fish, the sea, and people, is somehow different, and even better because Jesus overcame death and had a fish breakfast with his friends. Example:

   Lord, bless the food of our table this morning, as we begin to learn of your great love for us and our world; through Jesus Christ, who passed even through death to be with his friends again. Amen.

3. Finally, during the meal, your family could share some ideas about the ways Jesus is with us. Sometimes we don't recognize him, in much the same way that the disciples failed to recognize him on the shore at breakfast. Perhaps, for example, you have seen a glimpse of Jesus

   —in some unexpected visitor,
   —in the smile of a stranger,
   —in a call within you to do something that otherwise you would be afraid to do.

We can begin to see the spirit of Jesus in the quite ordinary events of our lives.

Easter—The Time Lasts All Year

SUNDAYS ARE EASTER DAYS

In the time of the Old Testament, the people of God kept the Sabbath as a day of rest. It meant they observed the Story of Creation's lesson: give thanks and know that what God has given is good. There was also a Sabbath year, the seventh year, a year of jubilee. During that year the fields remained unplanted and people ate of the surplus of previous years, thanking God and showing him that they believed in his providence: the years would be fertile years, and more crops would grow.

By the time of Jesus, the observance of the Sabbath was a very strict one. Not only was no work to be done, but Scribes and Pharisees kept watch and reprimanded the faithful for infractions of the rule. There are examples where Jesus and his disciples cured on the Sabbath, and were accused of working and, thus, breaking the law.

Because Jesus rose on a Sunday, Christians gradually came to observe their Sabbath as Sunday and it came to have a new meaning. Sunday was a day of rest, but it also came to be a day to share with family and friends, for it was on Sunday evening that Jesus appeared to his friends.

With your family, you might plan together how this year you might observe that same spirit of Sunday as a day of thanksgiving, joy, and a day to be with family and friends.

Sundays might be a time for you to:

—Go out to breakfast after your church service (eating out for families is much less costly at breakfast) or buy something special for breakfast;

—Visit friends and relatives;

—Go on picnics, go to parks, join in some simple family games;

—Write letters to friends and relatives;

—Remind yourselves of the resurrection and new life with fresh flowers on that day, a fresh tablecloth, and so forth;

—Observe the day of rest by an extra nap on that day—a time especially set aside to rest from the week's work and become renewed for the week to come.

Whatever you decide to do to keep holy the Lord's Day, do it as a family that rejoices in being Christian and celebrating weekly the new life of Christ.

THE EXPERIENCE OF RISING

To remember that Jesus rose from the dead, that he is risen and is now with us, is easy when we realize the many ways we experience risings. Steam rises from the stove, smoke from our campfire rises, our helium balloons rise, and we ourselves rise and shine when we are happy and rested. But the most obvious example of rising to children and to us is seen in the rising of bread. Baking bread together and watching it rise is a perfect family setting for talking about the rising of Jesus. Here is a recipe you can try and some conversations to have while you bake.

A Rye Dough Recipe—especially good for sculpturing bread into different shapes and forms

1 pack yeast	3 Tablespoons vinegar
1 cup warm water	1 teaspoon salt
1 Tablespoon brown sugar or honey	1 cup white flour (and more set aside for kneading)
1 Tablespoon oil	
2 cups light or dark rye flour	

—Pour the warm water (lukewarm, not hot) into a big bowl

—Sprinkle the yeast and sugar or honey into the water (in 5 minutes the yeast will form a scum with bubbles so you know it is alive and growing)

—Add oil and salt and half the flour

—When the dough gets too thick to stir with a spoon, turn it out onto a floured board, and with your hands work in as much flour as needed to be non-sticky yet springy.

—Form dough into a ball and oil it. Set it to rise in a covered bowl placed in a warm, draft-free place about an hour or until about double in size.

While you are waiting and watching every fifteen minutes or so, here are some things to talk about and think about, or even make posters or decorate paper plates with:

Bread is patience. How?
Bread makes itself. How?
Bread is the symbol of the staff of life. How?
Bread is labor. How?
Bread will grow, stretch, rise. How?
Bread is love. How?
Jesus is our bread. How? Why?

—When the dough is ready, punch it down and knead the air bubbles out. Add more flour if it's too sticky.

—Now begin to sculpture it.

EXAMPLES:

The Hands of Friendship: Divide the dough into 4 balls, flatten the balls into the shape of your hand. Put your hand on top and cut around your fingers to make another hand. When you have finished, put any two hands together like a handshake or a hand clasp of friendship.

The Butterfly's New Life: Roll some bread into the shape of a caterpillar and the rest into a butterfly to bake side by side. Decorate with pieces of dried fruit (such as raisins, currants, or dates).

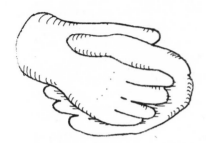

—Glaze the finished product with egg white or butter or milk. Put it on a greased cookie sheet and if it has risen enough bake it at 350° until golden brown (the amount of time depends upon the size of the pieces).

As you eat it, share a prayer of how Jesus is with us in the bread and in his rising.

Lord Jesus, as we watched the bread rise we are reminded that you did rise from your grave early Easter morning. May the rising of bread always be a sign to us of the greatness of your love and your promise to be always with us. Amen.

WHEN JESUS SAID GOODBYE

We remember that Jesus remained with his mother and friends after Easter. He continued to teach, to heal the sick, to feed the poor, and to pray with his disciples. The Church remembers this time of Jesus' ministry with nearly six weeks, called Eastertide. On the 40th day of this time, Christians gather together to celebrate Jesus' leaving, his ascension to be with his Father in heaven. We, too, as a family, can celebrate Ascension Day.

A Service for Remembering When Jesus Said Goodbye

1. Someone in your family can read the story, in Acts 1:1-11.

2. Share what you have said to your friends and those you love when you have left them. What do you say as you leave in the morning for school or for work? What do you say as you leave the home of a friend? What do you say as you go to bed at night?

3. Often we give one another a gift or a keepsake which will remind us of a special time together, or of a special place such as a vacation spot. A keepsake helps us to remember the person who gives it to us—a photograph, a ring, a flower, a book, or some souvenir. You can probably remember others that you have received or given to someone else. Ask each family member to bring out a keepsake or souvenir and share what it means to him or her.

4. The keepsake Jesus left with his friends was a special gift. He told them to do his work—to share what they knew, to feed and house the poor and hungry, to care for the sick—and he would send them the special gift of his spirit, his Holy Spirit. What signs remind you of the Holy Spirit? (Christians often think of a picture of a dove or flames of fire.) On Ascension Day make such a symbol of the Spirit to wear by:

—using shrinkable plastic, available at most toy stores,

—painting the design on a flat rock, and gluing a pin-back on the reverse side,

—using baker's dough.

Baker's Dough

Mix 1 cup flour, ½ cup salt, about ½ cup water to make stiff mixture.

Roll out the dough and cut with a cookie cutter, or shape by hand.

Make a hole in the top of each keepsake for hanging.

Place on a cookie sheet and bake in a 225° oven for several hours. When the keepsakes are cool, paint with poster paint which has been mixed with a little white glue to keep it from flaking. When the paint is dry spray the keepsake with acrylic sealer.

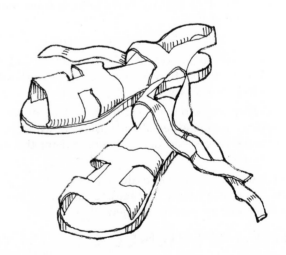